Traditional Islamic Ethics
The Concept of Virtue and its Implications
for Contemporary Human Rights

Irfaan Jaffer

Series in Philosophy of Religion

Copyright © 2022 Vernon Press, an imprint of Vernon Art and Science Inc, on behalf of the author.

All rights reserved. No part of this publication may be reproduced, stored in a retrieval system, or transmitted in any form or by any means, electronic, mechanical, photocopying, recording, or otherwise, without the prior permission of Vernon Art and Science Inc.

www.vernonpress.com

In the Americas:
Vernon Press
1000 N West Street, Suite 1200
Wilmington, Delaware, 19801
United States

In the rest of the world:
Vernon Press
C/Sancti Espiritu 17,
Malaga, 29006
Spain

Series in Philosophy of Religion

Library of Congress Control Number: 2021936395

ISBN: 978-1-64889-365-0

Also available: 978-1-64889-038-3 [Hardback]; 978-1-64889-278-3 [PDF, E-Book]

Cover design by Vernon Press. Cover image designed by visnezh / Freepik.

Product and company names mentioned in this work are the trademarks of their respective owners. While every care has been taken in preparing this work, neither the authors nor Vernon Art and Science Inc. may be held responsible for any loss or damage caused or alleged to be caused directly or indirectly by the information contained in it.

Every effort has been made to trace all copyright holders, but if any have been inadvertently overlooked the publisher will be pleased to include any necessary credits in any subsequent reprint or edition.

Table of contents

	Abstract	*v*
	Foreword	*vii*
	Preface	*ix*
	Acknowledgments	*xi*
Chapter 1	**Introduction**	1
	1.1. Approaching human rights and Islam	
	1.2. Speaking about Islam: the perennial school and Islamic traditionalism	
	1.3. A note on sources and terminology	
	1.4. Book outline	
	1.5. A note on translation, transliteration and structure	
Chapter 2	**Human Rights: The Incomplete Development of a Secular-Liberal Ethic**	19
	2.1. Popular human rights histories	
	2.2. The construction and assumptions of human rights histories	
Chapter 3	**Human Rights and Their Underlying Ethical Theories**	31
	3.1. A critical exploration of utilitarianism	
	3.2. A critical exploration of natural rights	
	3.3. A critical exploration of ethical sentimentalism	
	3.4. Human rights and the problem of universality	
Chapter 4	**Religion, Islam, and Human Rights**	57
	4.1. Islam and the challenge of human rights	
	4.2. Understanding contemporary Islamic thought	

4.3. The perennial school of thought and Islamic traditionalism

Chapter 5	**Traditional Islamic Ethics and the Concept of Virtue**	93

5.1. A Quranic perspective on morality and virtue

5.2. Traditional Islamic virtue theory

Chapter 6	**Virtue Theory and its Implications for Human Rights**	127

6.1. Human rights and the station of servanthood

6.2. Islamic law, pluralism, corporeal punishment, and gender

Chapter 7	**Conclusion**	153
	Bibliography	*159*
	Index	*169*

Abstract

This book is made up of two main parts. The first part argues that the dominant understanding and formulation of international human rights needs to be more flexible and inclusive in order to be truly universal in scope. This is because the Universal Declaration of Human Rights and its contemporary offshoots are still underpinned by the Western ethical tradition and its secular-liberal principles; therefore, they are at odds with other cultural traditions around the world and their respective value systems. To this end, the first section of this book critically engages with popular human rights histories that wrongly portray human rights as a linear and progressive ideology and the triumphant end to humanity's perennial search for justice. The first section then proceeds to critically engage with three popular ethical theories – utilitarianism, natural rights, and ethical sentimentalism – that claim to 'ground' or justify the existence of human rights. It concludes that all three theories are inconclusive and problematic. Thus, the goal of the first section of this book is to clear-out a space for dialogue by arguing that the exclusion of any alternative human rights theories is unwarranted.

After creating a space for dialogue, the second part of this book constructs a theory of virtue ethics that has the ability to 'ground' an Islamic vision of human rights. This is because virtue ethics addresses the fundamental questions concerning human existence that ultimately determine the constitution of particular rights. In order to answer these questions, this study operates within the framework of the perennial school of thought in the Islamic context. In doing so, it concludes that much of the friction between Islam and contemporary human rights is due to the fact that the latter emphasizes liberal understandings of concepts such as rights, freedom, and equality. In contrast, this book's theory of virtue ethics concludes that an Islamic human rights model must be grounded in God and His revelation; moreover, it must emphasize human duties, spiritual transformation, and social harmony. It also argues that an Islamic human rights society is one that is filled with 'reminders' of the Divine presence and structured in a way that allows Muslims to achieve their primary purpose in life – to serve and represent God in this world and felicity in the hereafter. Finally, the second section of the book concludes by offering some introductory remarks concerning contemporary human rights issues, such as the general implementation of Islamic law, religious pluralism, corporal punishment, and gender differences. It ultimately argues that there are spaces of convergence between the Islamic and the modern human rights traditions. However, it also argues that there are some fundamental differences that cannot be reconciled, and that these differences should be welcomed by human rights proponents.

Foreword

The charter of human rights was drafted in light of the horrendous events of World War II. Soon after the war ended, the Universal Declaration of Human Rights (UDHR) document was adopted by the United Nations General Assembly. However, there were many who disagreed with various points in the charter and viewed the whole notion as an imposition of Western values and standards on others, especially as its authority was located in "the conscience of mankind." The dictates of public conscience have been considered highly subjective. This is especially because notions of democracy, pluralism, and human rights have been discussed without taking into consideration communitarian interpretations and the possible ramifications for different communities and faith groups. Such actions are conceived by many as being culturally and religiously insensitive to different faith groups. As such, the UDHR has failed to appeal to diverse faith communities and traditions across the world, especially as many of the countries that appeal to human rights have continuously violated them.

The intersection of Islam and human rights has in recent times been discussed and debated by various scholars. Irfaan Jaffer's book is a welcome addition to the discourse. The author approaches the subject from a very different and unique perspective. He challenges the contemporary secular-liberal understanding of human rights and contends that the formulation of human rights needs to be more inclusive and ecumenical. Highlighting the problems of the secular-liberal tradition, Jaffer astutely demonstrates that the claim that a universal standard of morality can be known by measuring the consequences of common acts or rules cannot ground human rights in a way that allows the latter to be universal, equal, and inalienable. For him, international human rights cannot be considered universal or inclusive because they are rooted in the modern-liberal principles of universalism, individualism, and secularism.

Instead, Jaffer offers an alternative Islamic theory of virtue ethics and addresses its implications for human rights. The novelty of this work becomes evident as Jaffer carefully and meticulously explores an Islamic theory of ethics and human rights which, he believes, must be grounded in virtue ethics. Conceptually, this is important because virtue ethics asks the larger questions related to the meaning and purpose of life, and it is the answers to these questions that ultimately determine what people consider to be human rights. He situates this within the broader framework concerning the purpose of human existence.

His theory of virtue ethics addresses three fundamental issues: the nature of reality; the nature of the human being and the Divine-human relationship; and the cultivation of virtue. Jaffer's theory of virtue ethics maintains that God is the one and only reality, and 'all else' has an illusionary, transient, and/or derivative mode of existence. The theory also maintains that the goal of human beings is to use their free will to serve and represent God on Earth by various forms of moral and spiritual transformations. His approach leads him to conclude that human beings can be God's representatives only if they are able to cultivate virtue ethics rooted in the revelatory sources.

Jaffer's book opens a new window on how various interpretive strategies can be utilized to reconceptualize the notion of human rights based on virtue ethics. While such an approach might appear novel and confessional to some, it is bound to appeal to both Muslims and non-Muslims across the globe. The work is a valuable and welcome addition to the emerging literature on human rights discourse.

Liyakat Takim
McMaster University
May 2021

Preface

Traditional Islamic Ethics is based on my dissertation which I completed and successfully defended at York University in 2018. However, the book's beginnings can be traced back to 2012, when I first discovered the perennial school of thought and its intellectual figures, such as Rene Guenon, Martin Lings, and Seyyed Hossein Nasr. I believe that their work helped me approach the subject of Islam and ethics in a way that stays true to Islam's 1400-year-old intellectual tradition. This was important to me because much of the contemporary academic work on the subject of Islam and human rights tends to reduce Islam to its legal and social dimensions. I hope that this books functions as a corrective to this tendency since the social and legal aspects of Islamic thought can only be grasped in light of the Quran's perennial principles and Islam's intellectual and ethical ethos.

After 2018, I was able to reflect on my work through many conversations I had with my family, friends, students, and colleagues. I was also afforded the time to continue my research and refine my thought on the complex issues I deal with in this book. These years of reflection and research allowed me to submit a more concise and thorough manuscript for publication. I hope that this book is a welcome addition to the growing work on the subject of Islamic ethics and human rights.

Acknowledgments

I would like to thank my family and friends for their support and encouragement during the long and demanding process of writing this book. More specifically, I would like to thank my parents, Nusrat and Shenaz Jaffer; my siblings, Aadil Jaffer and Sara Champsi; my lovely wife Sayyeda Jaffer; and some of my dearest friends, Mark McGuire, Dr. Merin Shobhana Xavier, Anil Sinahroy, and Shiraz Khan. This undertaking would have been next to impossible without their seemingly endless supply of prayers, patience, encouragement, and dialogue.

Just as importantly, I would like to recognize some of my academic colleagues. My PhD supervisor, Professor Minoo Derayeh, put aside many hours of her valuable time in order to provide me with much-needed advice and constructive criticism. Professor Selma Zecevic selflessly guided me ever since I took her introductory course on Islam during my undergraduate studies over 15 years ago. I would also like to thank Professor Liyakat Takim for his comments on my work, as well as his extreme professionalism and kindness. Finally, I would like to acknowledge Professor Mojtaba Mahdavi who painstakingly read over my entire work and provided me with a comprehensive list of issues that I needed to address and/or clarify.

Thank you.

Chapter 1

Introduction

Human rights – as expressed in the International Bill of Rights – are increasingly envisioned as a set of self-evident and foundational truths. In turn, many human rights advocates and organizations are treating them as *the* social and legal norm for the global community. However, despite this growing popularity, it is clear that human rights are far from self-evident or foundational. Rather, they are symptomatic in so far as they are derived from a particular worldview and the latter's basic metaphysical, ontological, and epistemological suppositions. More specifically, today's human rights are a product of the secular-liberal ethical tradition and have their roots in Christian natural law; therefore, they cannot be qualified as 'universal'. If this fact is consistently ignored, there will continue to be growing friction and resistance from other cultural traditions around the world. These traditions will carry on seeing human rights as an alien concept that is being employed as a tool for Western or Global imperialism.[1] In light of this, I argue that the formulation and implementation of human rights needs to be more inclusive and decentralized respectively. It needs to open up a space for different human rights visions that share the same goal of protecting citizens, and helping them pursue their society's particular vision of 'the good'. This approach would lead to an 'after-the-fact' or 'accidental' overlapping consensus of rights, and it is only these rights that could fairly be described as 'universal'. However, many theorists, such as Jack Donnelly and Michael Ignatieff, are quick to dismiss religion in general, and Islam in particular, as a potential source for human rights. For example, Donnelly writes that "Muslims are indeed regularly and forcefully called upon…to treat other with respect and dignity…[However,] these injunctions…appeal to Divine commands that establish duties, not (human) rights.[2] According to Ignatieff, "In Islamic eyes, universalizing rights discourse implies a sovereign and

---

[1] There is a debate concerning imperialism and its 'location of power' in an increasingly globalized and technological world. For a more detailed approach to this debate and its related concepts, see Ania Loomba, *Colonialism/Postcolonialism*, 2nd ed. (New York: Routledge, 2005).
[2] Jack Donnelly, *Universal Human Rights: In Theory and Practice*, 2nd ed. (New York: Cornell University Press, 2003), 73.

discrete individual, which is blasphemous from the perspective of the Koran."[3] The reason for this dismissal of religion is a matter of both theory and practice. In theory, human rights discourse in the West has shifted from the religious sphere to the political and legal sphere; thus, it is in friction with any discourse that is theological in nature. Related to this is the supposed dominance of (liberal) reason in the public sphere, and its assumption that any dialogue based on revelation and belief is outdated and primitive.[4] Indeed, John Rawls – who is normally accredited for the revival of modern liberalism – held that the public sphere, particularly in the area of politics, should be reserved for language that only 'reasonable' people would endorse.[5] Of course, delineating what is 'universally reasonable' is problematic, and I critically examine this problem throughout this book. In practice, Islam is generally considered responsible for many human rights abuses such as the female genital mutilation (FGM) taking place in Africa and in the Middle East; the penal code implemented in areas such as Afghanistan and Saudi Arabia; and the 9/11 attacks carried out on US soil.

1.1. Approaching human rights and Islam

The apparent roadblock between human rights and Islam is unfortunate. It is almost impossible to deny the positive potential that the religion and its one billion plus adherents have in advancing human rights. This is especially the case when one considers the significance that Islamic normative texts, such as the Quran and hadith literature, place on establishing justice on earth and the rich 1400-year-old intellectual tradition that accompanies that Divine imperative.[6] For example, the Quran reads:

> O you who have faith! Be maintainers of justice and witnesses for the sake of Allah, even if it should be against yourselves, or [your] parents and near relatives, and whether it be [someone] rich or poor, for Allah has a greater right over them. So do not follow [your] desires, lest you

---

[3] Michael Ignatieff, "The Attack on Human Rights," *Foreign Affairs* 80, no. 6 (November 2001): 103-4.
[4] The modern resurgence of the liberal belief in the 'secular-rational human' is normally traced back to John Rawls and his seminal work: John Rawls, *A Theory of Justice* (London: Oxford University Press, 1971).
[5] John Rawls, "The Laws of People," *Critical Inquiry* 20, no. 1 (Autumn 1993): 33-68.
[6] For an overview of the Islamic intellectual tradition's approach to justice, see Majid Khadduri, *The Islamic Conception of Justice* (Baltimore: John Hopkins University Press, 1984).

should be unfair, and if you distort [the testimony] or disregard [it], Allah is indeed aware of what you do. (4:135)[7]

It is true that a human rights scheme that is rooted in revelation, Islamic history, and traditional norms may not sit well with the secular-liberal tradition and its advocates. However, there is no 'white man's burden', and there is no duty on those in power to impose what it deems to be good on other peoples. If there is a burden, then it is the 'human burden', and that is to take the time to understand the 'Other' and not accept or reject their beliefs for them. This is why this study is primarily dialogical in nature. Irene Oh aptly describes the benefits of a dialogical approach in writing that

> The dialogical model aids with understanding persons from different traditions, and cultures than one's own because it recognizes those persons as agents like oneself...To understand others as agents requires that we view them as possessing self-understanding rather than unilaterally categorize them as mere objects of study... In dialogue that promotes understanding, others have voices, and we are required over the course of conversation to acknowledge and respond to those voices. Moreover, and just as important, we recognize through such dialogue our own assumptions, the limits of our knowledge, and the possibilities for understanding, and we therefore present human faces to our interlocutors.[8]

In terms of human rights, I enter the dialogue as part of the pluralist-universal school of thought which attempts to negotiate a middle position between the extremes of universalism and cultural relativism. This position is based on the understanding that cultural traditions are both unique and similar. They are unique insofar as they work within particular worldviews and develop according to their own particular socio-historical contexts, and they are similar insofar as they are human collectivities that develop with common tendencies that are grounded in a shared humanity. In light of this, I argue that all peoples should be free to develop their own human rights models. As mentioned, my working assumption is that this approach will lead to an 'after-the-fact' or 'accidental' minimal overlapping consensus of rights, and it is these rights that can truly be described as 'universal'. In particular, I

---

[7] 'Ali Quli Qara'i, trans., *The Qur'an: With a Phrase-by-Phrase Translation* (New York: Tahrike Tarsile Qur'an Inc., 2006).
[8] Irene Oh, *The Rights of God: Islam, Human Rights, and Comparative Ethics* (Washington: Georgetown University Press, 2007), 7.

am concerned with the relationship between human rights and Islam in light of the newly emerging religious typography which is characterized by the so-called 'religious resurgence' and contemporary Islamist movements.[9] It is true that colonization, globalization, and the pervasiveness of liberalism have replaced traditional Islamic societies with Muslim-majority nation-states. Nevertheless, many Muslims in these nation-states, and around the world, are increasingly looking to 'Islamic ideals' in their attempts at reform, and in their understanding of current international human rights. For this reason, I argue in favor of the inclusion of human rights models grounded in sacred religious texts and the Islamic intellectual tradition. To this end, I develop an Islamic theory of virtue ethics and address the theory's general implications for human rights. Thus, this book focuses more-so on ethical theory than human rights as such; this is because the former is the starting point and foundation of the latter. Moreover, it focuses on virtue ethics because virtue situates morality within a broader framework of discourse; instead of asking about the right way to act, it begins by asking about the right way to 'be'. Therefore, virtue ethics is concerned with right action in light of questions concerning the nature of reality; the nature of the human being and Divine-human relationship; and the cultivation of virtue.[10] It is the answers to these questions that ultimately determine what people understand and accept as human rights.

1.2. Speaking about Islam: the perennial school and Islamic traditionalism

I develop my theory of virtue ethics within the theoretical framework of the perennial school of thought. Perennialism developed in the twentieth century with the work of its 'founders', Ananda Coomaraswamy (d.1947) and Rene Guenon (d.1951).[11] This school of thought is primarily concerned with explaining the concept of 'tradition' in light of the modern world and its ideologies. For perennialists, "tradition implies both the Sacred as revealed to humanity through revelation and the unfolding and development of that sacred message in the history of the particular human community for which it was

---

[9] Peter L. Berger, "The Desecularization of the World: A Global Overview," in *The Desecularization of the World: Resurgent Religion and World Politics*, ed. Peter L. Berger (Washington: Ethics and Public Policy Center, 1999), 1-18.
[10] For an introduction to virtue ethics, see Daniel C. Russell, ed., *The Cambridge Companion to Virtue Ethics* (New York: Cambridge University Press, 2013).
[11] Other earlier and significant figures include Titus Burckhardt (d.1984), Marco Pallis (d.1989), Frithjof Schuon (d.1998) and Martin Lings (d. 2005).

Introduction 5

destined."[12] In light of this, perennialism's central doctrine is that all revelations originate from the same source and contain the same perennial truths. Moreover, they argue that these revelations and their respective religions grounded and shaped virtually every civilization before the rise and influence of modernity. They inspired all human activity, ranging from religious doctrine and law, to architecture, music, and calligraphy. Moreover, these revelations functioned to construct a general and common worldview that was centered around the Divine and the Divine-human relationship.[13] Thus, perennialists understand premodern religious traditions as both unique and similar. They are unique because they flowered in different spacio-temporal contexts, and they emphasize different aspects of the Divine.[14] On the other hand, premodern religious traditions are similar due to their common essence – in *divinnis* – and in their expression of the same perennial truths.[15,16]

In this book, I speak about Islam from the perspective of the perennial school and I refer to this perspective as 'Islamic traditionalism'. Moreover, I refer to those who adhere to this point of view as 'Muslim traditionalists'.[17]

According to the latter, all premodern Islamic societies belonged to a single Islamic tradition because they were all rooted in the Quran and expressed the latter's underlying and universal principles – albeit in different ways and to different degrees. For example, Seyyed Hossein Nasr applies the perennial perspective to Islam and writes:

> Two centuries ago, if Westerners...were to study Islam, they would have encountered but a single Islamic tradition. Such persons could have detected numerous schools of thought...[and] interpretations... But all

---

[12] Seyyed Hossein Nasr, *Islam in the Modern World: Challenged by the West, Threatened by Fundamentalism, Keeping Faith with Tradition* (New York: HarperOne, 2007), 3.
[13] For an introduction and overview to the perennial school, see Martin Lings and Clinton Minnaar, ed., *The Underlying Religion: An Introduction to the Perennial Philosophy* (Bloomington: World Wisdom, 2007).
[14] Nevertheless, these differences are understood as providential because they allow for the salvation of different 'types' of people.
[15] Perennialists consider modern societies as an exception to this rule. That is, they argue that the underlying principles of premodern and modern societies are incompatible *on a whole*. However, as this study shows in the case of human rights, there are still areas of convergence where agreement can be reached.
[16] See chapter 4 for a more in-depth explanation of the perennial school and its approach to religion.
[17] Some contemporary Muslim traditionalists include S.H. Nasr, William Chittick, Joseph Lumbard, and Reza Shah-Kazemi.

that they could have observed...would have belonged in one degree or another to the Islamic tradition; that is, to that single tree of Divine Origin whose roots are the Quran and the...Ḥadīth, and whose trunk and branches constitute that body of tradition that has grown from those roots over some fourteen centuries in nearly every inhabited quarter of the globe.[18]

Thus, Islamic traditionalism is the perennial school's particular explanation of the Islamic intellectual tradition as a whole – that is, 1400-years of Islamic theological, philosophical, and mystical thought – and the ways in which this tradition manifested the Quran's underlying metaphysical, ontological, and epistemological principles. More specifically, Muslim traditionalists explain Islam by focusing on what Sachicko Murara and William Chittick describe as the 'highpoints' or 'landmarks' of the Islamic intellectual tradition. This refers to the great and influential Islamic thinkers and texts that explained the original vision of the Quran and Islam in accordance with the needs of their respective times.[19] It is important to remember that I focus more on the 'original vision' or 'underling unity' of Islamic thought rather than on its formal, outward, and expressive differences. This is in order to keep line with my goal of approaching the religion holistically for the sake of dialogue. Therefore, it is this particular understanding of Islam that I use to critically explore contemporary Islamic thought and construct a theory of virtue ethics. Moreover, it is in this context that I use terms such as 'Quranic worldview', 'Islamic ethos', 'Muslim mentality' and the like. For example, from the perspective of Islamic traditionalism, the term 'Quranic worldview' refers to the essential Quranic ideas about the reality of the world which Muslims have held and elaborated on for centuries. For instance, this includes the Quranic concept of life after death and the 'day of judgment'. In this regard, I assume that the perennial concept of the hereafter is one of the many concepts that influence the general Muslim outlook and approach to life, that is, the basic 'Muslim mentality' and its respective manifestations. To be clear, some Muslims find Islamic traditionalism problematic, and, in some cases, the school is rejected by the same Muslims that it claims to represent. However, this is not problematic to the extent that this book only claims to 'speak for' those Muslims who accept Islamic traditionalism, that is, Muslim

---

[18] Nasr, *Islam in the Modern World*, 1.
[19] Sachiko Murata and William C. Chittick, *The Vision of Islam* (Minnesota: Paragon House, 1994), x.

traditionalists, and those Muslims who are most closely represented by this perspective despite any differences of opinion.[20]

There are several reasons why I have situated this book within the framework of Islamic traditionalism. First, it approaches Islam in the unified and holistic manner necessary for any dialogical approach. Second, Islamic traditionalism addresses the basic questions of human existence that need to be answered in order to form any theory of virtue ethics and concomitant human rights model. Third, it accepts virtually all of Islam's 1400-year-old intellectual tradition; therefore, it understands Muslims as agents with self-understanding and the right to determine and pursue their own vision of 'the good'. Fourth, members of the perennial school generally belong to a single religious form; thus, they speak as 'insiders' from their respective religions. This means that Muslim traditionalists are practicing Muslims that adhere to the tenants and practices of the Islamic faith.[21] Finally, this book assumes that Islamic traditionalism – despite the pervasiveness of modern ideologies – still represents the general intellectual and behavioral orientation of many Muslims today. To reiterate, this school of thought represents just one of the many Muslim voices concerned with the issue of Islam, modernity, and human rights. Nevertheless, I believe it is a substantial and important voice – and one that is underrepresented in Western academic institutions. Thus, drawing on Islamic traditionalism is important because many 'progressive' Muslim academics seem to underestimate, or wrongly assume, that they can circumvent the importance that Muslims place on their traditional heritage as a whole. Thus, they often construct theories that are alien to the Muslim mentality, and the net result is that their thought is ignored or condemned. Moreover, the authors of these works are sometimes perceived as ignorant or willing puppets for Western or Global powers. For example, Abdal Hakim Murad – a prominent and popular Muslim intellectual figure – reviews Esack Farid's work and writes:

---

[20] For a response to common critiques against the perennial school see Charles Upton, "What is a 'Traditionalist'? – Some Clarifications," Sacred Web: A Journal of Tradition and Modernity, accessed July 25, 2017, http://www.sacredweb.com/online_articles/sw 17_upton.html

[21] In my opinion, an 'insider' perspective is needed in order to fully comprehend a religious tradition because the latter is a lived reality and not a constructed ideology. However, this issue is beyond the scope of this study. For an overview, see Russell T. McCutcheon, ed., *The Insider/Outsider Problem in the Study of Religion: A Reader* (New York: The Bath Press, 1999).

The age-old European concern with securing the Europeanization of the earth – imperialism, to use a more frank expression – today relies on reshaping the parameters accepted by the Other: accession to Western values can only be guaranteed when non-Westerners think in Western terms. Among secular thinkers this is today a common transformation, but in Esack's case, his tutors have successfully secured a more interesting paradigm shift of a *theological* order... His book...completely lacks the style and reverent tenor of Muslim reflection, with its characteristic indigenous terminology, and with the deployment of scriptures as sacred archetypes rather than archaic problems.[22,23]

In this light, I argue that any method that historicizes or simply ignores the multifaceted aspects of the Islamic tradition, such as the hadith literature or Sufi metaphysics, will remain alien to Muslims; therefore, it will fail in its goal of reform.

One of Islamic traditionalism's greatest strengths is its ability to navigate Islam's remarkable plurality without negating its essential unity.[24] However, since this book focuses on Islam's 'essential unity', it is necessary to briefly address the popular postmodern and post-colonial critique concerning 'essentialism'.[25] This is because many contemporary academic works concerned with 'Islamic reform' have adopted this style of critique and claim that there is no way to meaningful way to speak about Islam as a single and unified tradition. Here, two important points need to be made. First, an extreme anti-essentialist stance is a counterproductive response to dangerous stereotypical generalizations, typified by works such as Samuel Huntington's

---

[22] Abdal-Hakim Murad, "Book Review of Farid Esack's Qur'an, Liberation and Pluralism," Muslim View: Reimagining British Muslims, accessed February 14, 2018, http://masud.co.uk/ISLAM/ahm/esack.htm.
[23] This is a review of: Farid Esack, *Qur'an, Liberation and Pluralism: An Islamic Perspective of Interreligious Solidarity Against Oppression* (Oxford: Oneworld Publications, 1997).
[24] Perennialism is sometimes critiqued for producing an inadequate account of religious differences. However, it seems that this critique is based on a misunderstanding of the school's theory of the transcendent unity of religions. Moreover, the perennial school opposes the modern academic trend of hyper-contextualization and hyper-specialization. Thus, its intellectual approach can be understood as a corrective to the general methodologies applied in the humanities and social sciences today.
[25] For an overview of postmodernism see Charles E. Winquist and Victor E. Taylor, ed., *Encyclopedia of Postmodernism* (New York: Routledge, 2001). For an overview of post-colonialism see Bill Ashcroft, Gareth Griffiths, and Helen Tiffin, ed., *Post-Colonial Studies: The Key Concepts*, 2nd ed. (New York: Routledge, 2000).

Clash of Civilizations and Benjamin Barber's *Jihad Versus McWorld*.[26] It is counterproductive because instead of attempting to construct solutions to real issues, it pre-emptively puts an end to any meaningful discussion and positive change. This is because postmodern and post-colonial thought generally argues that 'truth' is relative to a subject's point of view; therefore, it maintains that subjects are limited by, and even products of, their particular societies' systems of ideology, discourse, and language. Thus, a person's truth claim does not represent any reality beyond the limited self.[27] For example, in terms of subjectivity, Tammy Clewell writes that

> Despite diverse and sometimes oppositional formulations, postmodernist and poststructuralist critics share an impulse to "deconstruct" the humanist subject as the intended source of knowledge and meaning. Such accounts redefine the human self as an entity constructed by, and not simply reflected in a culture's social discourses, linguistic structures, and signifying practices.[28]

Al Hassan Zaidi articulates the problem with this type of approach by quoting Marcel Gauchet and writing the following:

> 'a global orientation on behalf of smallness, plurality, and marginality, accompanied by the proliferation of specializations and the bureaucratic explosion of scholarship'[29] does not necessarily render the Other more accessible and understandable. It may, in fact, serve only to further

---

[26] See Samuel Huntington, *The Clash of Civilizations and the Remaking of World Order* (India: Penguin Books, 1997). Also see Benjamin Barber, *Jihad vs. McWorld: Terrorism's Challenge to* Democracy (New York: Random House, 2010).

[27] Of course, postmodernism and post-colonialism are two different schools of thought with considerable differences between and within each school. However, a general critique is necessary since both schools – in line with their underlying assumption and approaches – are notoriously difficult to 'pin down'. Thus, in general, it can fairly be stated that they both share a common tendency towards anti-universal particularism through the use of socio-historical deconstructionism.

[28] Tammy Clewell, "Subjectivity," in *Encyclopedia of Postmodernism*, ed. Charles E. Winquist and Victor E. Taylor (New York: Routledge, 2001), 382.

[29] Marcel Gauchet, *The Disenchantment of the World: A Political History of Religion*, trans. Oscar Burge (Princeton, Princeton University press, 1997), 17.

mystify the Other by highlighting the Other's internal indeterminacy, differences and heterogeneity.[30]

On this view of subjectivity, there is no possibility of cross-cultural understanding and no method of furthering the cause of peace and justice on a global scale. Moreover, this understanding is largely alien to Islamic intellectual tradition and its general belief that human beings share a similar essence (*fiṭrah*), and that they have the ability to gradually transcend the relative realm and come to know the Absolute. Related to this is the Islamic intellectual tradition's particular emphasis on the connection between truth and justice. In general, it is only when one knows the truth, that is, the reality of a thing in relation to the whole, that one can implement justice, that is, put that thing in its right place. Along with being counterproductive, the second point is that an extreme anti-essentialist stance is also intellectually nonsensical. Simply put, this is because anti-essentialism is an essential claim itself, and, therefore, it falls victim to its own premise. It is stuck with the age-old problem of relativism: the contradictory and illogical claim that everything is relative except the relative. Frithjof Schuon clearly elucidated this problem by writing the following:

> In short, every idea is reduced to a relativity of some sort, whether psychological, historical, or social; but the assertion nullifies itself by the fact that it too presents itself as a psychological, historical, or social relativity. The assertion nullifies itself if it is true and by nullifying itself logically proves thereby that it is false; its initial absurdity lies in the implicit claim to be unique in escaping, as if by enchantment, from a relativity that is declared to be the only possibility.[31]

My response to the dangers of over-generalizations is careful and qualified generalizations. The latter is worth the risk because it is only holistic accounts that can satisfy the human need for meaning, understanding, and dialogue. In this regard, Gauchet writes the following:

> Let me assure the reader that I recognize the dangers of this enterprise...I am aware of the damage caused by the "ideas of totality." My sole excuse for deliberately taking these risks is the need to

---

[30] Ali Hassan Zaidi, "Islam, Modernity and the Human Sciences: Toward a Dialogical Approach" (PhD diss., York University, 2007), 4-5.
[31] Frithjof Schuon, *Logic and Transcendence: A New Translation with Selected Letters*, ed. James Cutsinger (Bloomington: World Wisdom, 2009), 6.

understand and my conviction that these risks must be taken. This does not mean we should yield to the lures of speculation, but that we should respond critically to the need for meaning whose main victims are those who naively believe they have freed themselves from that need.[32]

Finally, I have chosen the framework of Islamic traditionalism because, despite the school's prolific corpus of work, there are very few comprehensive studies that have been carried out on the subject of Islamic ethics and human rights. Therefore, this book is also an attempt to fill this lacuna of inquiry. In doing so, it is important to note that this book is not intended to be a work on Islamic law. This is because I argue that the Islamic legal tradition is grounded in the basic metaphysical, ontological, and epistemological principles of the Islamic intellectual tradition. Thus, it is the latter that needs to be critically explored in relation to any study concerned with Islamic ethics, modernity, and human rights.[33]

1.3. A note on sources and terminology

I develop my theory of Islamic virtue ethics by drawing on the thought of Muslim traditionalists such as Rene Guenon, Martin Lings, S. H. Nasr, William Chittick, Reza-Shah Kazemi and others. At the same time, in order to demonstrate that this particular perspective is indeed rooted in the Islamic intellectual tradition, I also draw on two primary sources. The first and most important source is the Quran – Islam's sacred and central text. According to Muslims, the Quran is the verbatim word of God that was revealed to the Prophet Muhammad over a span of twenty-three years (709-732 C.E.). Muslims generally understand the Quran as a perfect source of guidance for both their individual and collective lives. Moreover, according to Fazlur Rahman's *Islam and Modernity*,

> ...the Qurʾānic revelation...lasted for just over twenty-two years, during which period all kinds of decisions on policy in peace and in war, on legal and moral issues in private and public life were made in the face of actual situations; thus, the Qurʾān had from the time of its revelation a practical and political application... This naturally encouraged the Muslim jurists and intellectuals to look up the Qurʾān (and model of the Prophet) as a unique repository of answers to all

---

[32] Gauchet, *Disenchantment of the World*, 17.
[33] The same is also true of current human rights law which is a product of the secular-liberal ethical tradition and its underlying principles and assumptions.

sorts of questions. That this approach succeeded in practice further strengthened the original belief of the Muslims in the efficacy of the revelation in providing true answers to virtually all situations.[34]

The second primary source is the thought of one of Islam's most significant intellectual figures, ʿAlī b. Abī Ṭālib – the fourth rightly guided Sunni caliph and the first Shia Imam.[35] I have chosen Imam Ali as a primary source because he is accepted as an authoritative figure by virtually all Muslims and a representative *par excellence* of the Islamic intellectual tradition. Nevertheless, there is disagreement concerning the reliability of the sources attributed to him. For example, this book draws on his famous collection of sayings and sermons known as *Nahj al-Balāgha* (*The Peak of Eloquence*).[36] This collection of work is generally considered authentic by the Shia world but inauthentic by most of the Sunni world. However, in relation to this study, the authenticity of *The Peak* is inconsequential.[37] This is because the Imam's thought is situated within the framework of Islamic traditionalism and the latter's focus on Islam's underlying unity means that the same ideas can be found in the thought of any figure that is part of the religion's intellectual tradition.[38] For the same reason, this work should not be considered exclusively Sunni or Shia in nature; rather, it is inclusive of both schools of thought and their various expressions throughout Islamic history.

In this book, I also tackle the issue of human rights terminology in general, and its use across cultures and in a global context in particular. Certain human rights terms, such as freedom and equality, are fraught with cultural-specific assumptions; however, they have come to possess an unquestionable authority. In the eyes of many human rights advocates, these words possess a sacred quality; therefore, they are beyond the scope of any serious critical

---

[34] Fazlur Rahman, *Islam and Modernity: Transformation of an Intellectual Tradition* (Chicago: Chicago University press, 1982), 2.
[35] Here on out referred to as Imam Ali or the Imam.
[36] Here on out referred to as *The Peak*. See Yasin T. Al-Jibouri, ed., *Peak of Eloquence: Nahjul-Balagha*, 7th ed. (New York: Tahrike Tarsile Quran Inc., 2009).
[37] Nevertheless, for a 'defense' of the authenticity of *The Peak*, see the prologue in Reza Shah-Kazemi, *Justice and Remembrance: Introducing the Spirituality of Imam Ali* (London: I.B. Tauris Publishers, 2007). Also see chapter three in S. H. M. Jafri, *The Political and Moral Vision of Islam* (New York: Tahrike Tarsile Quran Inc, 2009).
[38] For example, William Chittick uses the framework of Islamic traditionalism to explore the thought of Rūmī, ibn ʿArabī, and Mulla Sadrā. In this regard, see: William Chittick, *In Search of the Lost Heart: Explorations in Islamic Thought*, ed. Mohammed Rustom, Atif Khalil and Kazuyo Murata (New York: State University of New York Press, 2012).

inquiry. However, the term 'equality' for example, carries the secular-liberal assumption that all types of equality – gender, race, class, and the like – are the same. To deny one is to deny them all and, hence, to be an enemy of human rights and progress. Uwe Poerkson's work critically examines these types of terms and argues that they are 'plastic words'. That is, they are words that gain prominence by being "transmitted into science or some other higher sphere, where they pick up the semblance of generally applicable truths. Then they wander back, authorized and canonized, into the vernacular, where they become dominant myths and overshadow everyday life."[39] According to Poerkson, these words are actually meaningless. He writes that

> The precise meaning of plastic words cannot be discerned. All words have many shifting meanings. But, through context, an author can be precise about which connotation of the word is being used. In contrast, authors have no powers of definition over plastic words; they are general, autonomous, vague and toneless."[40]

Thus, it can be argued that the concept of 'equality' gains its authority from the field of mathematics where it is used as a specific quantitative-value term, but it lacks any specific meaning when used in the general vernacular as a vague qualitative-value term. What happens when these plastic words are manufactured and consistently employed? Sherman Jackson rightly describes this situation by pointing out that

> ...the real power of American whiteness lays in its effective invisibility. While Hispanics, Asians, blacks and others are immediately recognized as raced, whites enjoy the presumption of being just "humans." This raises their perspective above critique, since it presents it as being above the biases and limitations of any particular history, ideology or culture. This in turn allows whites to speak for "humanity" as a whole... This...is also the secret behind the power and pervasiveness of liberalism today. Words like "freedom," "equality," "reason," "tolerance" are commonly used without the slightest understanding or hint that their users are invoking liberal freedom, liberal equality, liberal reason or liberal tolerance. Faced with these deployments, Muslims often find themselves debilitated by the feeling that they are fighting a losing battle, stuck in a perpetual mode of apology, hopelessly strengthening

---

[39] Uwe Poerkson, *Plastic Words: The Tyranny of a Modular Language*, trans. Jutta Mason and David Cayley (Pennsylvania: The Pennsylvania University State Press, 1995), 4.
[40] Poerkson, *Plastic Words*, 8.

and reinforcing their inquisitors' indictments with every would-be response...[41]

In light of this, I pay extra careful attention to human rights terminology by precisely defining certain 'key words' and their underlying assumptions. Without this kind of analysis, it would be impossible to engage in productive cross-cultural dialogue.

1.4. Book outline

In chapter two, I critically explore popular human rights histories. This undertaking is important for two interconnected reasons. The first is that histories in general are not an impartial account of past events, communities, and people.[42] Rather, they are constructs that are influenced by a particular historian's underlying beliefs and assumptions. Thus, popular human rights histories are largely written by those who assume human rights are a positive, progressive, and inevitable stage in the unfolding of human history. They present the Universal Declaration of Human Rights and its offshoots as necessary and valid for all peoples. In many cases, they also contrast human rights with religion and generally 'describe' the latter as an oppressive and incompatible belief system. The second reason that critical analysis is necessary is because these histories are not simply related to understanding the past; they affect people's understanding and actions in the present. Many advocates of 'humanitarian intervention' base their intellectual justification on popular human rights histories.[43] For this reason, these accounts need to be demystified in order to open up a space for different human rights visions, particularly for visions that are not rooted in the secular-liberal tradition. Therefore, in chapter two, I analyze several dubious assumptions that are common to popular human rights histories, and I argue that these assumptions are misleading and unwarranted.

In chapter three, I carefully consider the contemporary debate about the foundation of human rights. This debate is about whether or not there is an

---

[41] Sherman Jackson, "Liberalism and the American Muslim Predicament," The Islamic Monthly, June 27, 2018, https://www.theislamicmonthly.com/liberalism-and-the-american-muslim-predicament/.

[42] On the issue of power and the construction of history, see Michel-Rolph Trouillot, *Silencing the Past: Power and the Production of History* (Boston: Beacon Press, 1995).

[43] In many cases, 'humanitarian intervention' simply acts as a means to justify the economic and political exploitation of 'Southern' nation-states. Again, the subject of human rights and economics is beyond the scope of this paper.

ethical theory that is able to 'ground' or justify the existence of human rights. More specifically, it asks: on what basis do human beings have rights and what exactly are those rights? In this chapter, I examine three main schools of thought on the issue: utilitarianism, natural rights, and ethical sentimentalism. In doing so, I argue that none of the ethical theories provide a satisfactory answer to the questions at hand. It is important to note that I purposefully leave aside religion as a possible justification for human rights. This is in order to highlight the fact that even within the Western liberal tradition itself there is no agreement on the existence or substance of rights. For this reason, I argue that (1) the imposition of human rights on a global scale is a form of imperialism, and (2) the exclusion of alternative human rights models based on sacred texts and religious norms is unjustified.

In chapter four, I look at the issue of human rights and religion in general, and human rights and Islam in particular. In terms of human rights and Islam, I discuss the apparent friction between the two ideologies in the areas of Islamic law, corporeal punishment, non-Muslims, and gender. After discussing this friction, I proceed to explore some of the different contemporary Muslim responses to these issues and, in doing so, I classify them into four general trends: fundamentalist, liberal, progressive, and traditionalist. I argue that it is the traditionalist approach that carries the most potential for honest and genuine change; therefore, I conclude the chapter by situating the school of thought and its approach to religion within the larger framework of religious studies.[44]

In chapter five, I develop a theory of virtue ethics by drawing on the school of Islamic traditionalism, as well as the Quran and thought of Imam Ali. In doing so, I explore three fundamental ideas: the nature of reality; the nature of the human being and the Divine-human relationship; and the cultivation of virtue. Ultimately, I argue that Muslims are servants and representatives of God and that they are tasked with following the revealed law and cultivating virtue. Thus, I contend that both revelation and virtue must be the focus of any moral theory that is properly grounded in the Islamic tradition, and the basis for any Islamic theory of human rights.

In chapter six, I discuss the implications of my virtue theory in terms of human rights. In doing so, I maintain that Muslims primarily understand themselves as responsible to God for their beliefs and actions. The net result is that their worldview emphasizes duties, inward freedom, and harmony over

---

[44] Here, 'honest and genuine' change means that any changes within the framework of Islamic traditionalism would remain faithful to premodern Islamic tradition as a whole.

that of rights, outward freedom, and equality respectively. Therefore, in this chapter, I argue that an Islamic human rights society is one that is centered around the Sacred and functions to help human beings achieve their primary purpose in life as servants and representatives of God. I conclude this chapter by exploring the implications of virtue theory in relation to the human rights issues of Islamic law, corporeal punishment, non-Muslims, and gender. It is important to note that these are introductory remarks because my main concern is to identify the parameters within which an Islamic theory of human rights can function. In any case, I argue that contemporary human rights are only partially compatible with the Islamic intellectual tradition and its worldview. Therefore, in line with the pluralist-universal school of human rights, my working assumption is that there is a minimal overlapping consensus between the two traditions, and that any differences should be welcomed by human rights advocates.

Finally, I conclude this book with a summary of its main points and reiterate the argument that the global implementation of human rights rooted in the secular-liberal tradition is a form of imperialism. For this reason, contemporary human rights need to be more inclusive, decentralized, and regulated if they are to work as a catalyst for positive change. Otherwise, they will continue to be another ideology used by those in power to further their own socio-political and economic agendas.

1.5. A note on translation, transliteration and structure

In concluding these introductory remarks, a brief note on translation, transliteration, and style is necessary. I use 'Ali Quli Qara'i's translation of the Quran unless otherwise noted.[45] Moreover, I frequently draw on *The Study Quran*'s comprehensive commentary of Quranic verses.[46] The latter is of particular importance because its methodology is in line with this book's focus on a holistic Islam that is explained by way of the Islamic intellectual tradition and its fundamental principles. In this regard, Nasr, the editor-in-chief, states,

> Although we have relied heavily upon traditional sources…we have also consulted reliable sources based on both previous and recent academic scholarship in Quranic studies. We have, moreover, carried out this task with constant awareness of the biases and fashions

---

[45] *The Qur'an.*
[46] Seyyed Hossein Nasr et al., eds., *The Study Quran: A New Translation and Commentary* (New York: HarperOne, 2015).

present in both historical and contemporary writings... We have been fully aware that many of these resources suffer...from the fact that they do not accept the Quran as revelation, they have a truncated view of the Islamic intellectual tradition, or they reject the Islamic worldview as a whole.[47]

Thus, *The Study Quran* draws on the Quranic commentary of seminal figures such as Fakhr al- Dīn al-Rāzī (d.1210), ʿUmar ibn Kathīr (d.1373), Muḥammad Ḥusayn Ṭabāṭabāʾī (d.1981), and others.[48]

The quoted primary sources are separated from the main body of the text as block quotations so that the reader can find them easily. Moreover, any changes in emphasis or translation are accounted for in the footnotes.

Finally, I have decided to forgo the use of transliteration for some of the Arabic terminology. This is because many Arabic/Islamic terms, such as Quran, Shia, Sunni, and shariah, are becoming part and parcel of the English language. Moreover, this decision is also based on the fact that this book is not solely a work in Islamic studies; it is interdisciplinary in nature and it includes the fields of human rights, equity studies, and ethical philosophy.

---

[47] Nasr et al., *The Study Quran*, xiv.
[48] For the comprehensive list, see Nasr et al., *The Study Quran*, lvii-lix.

Chapter 2

Human Rights: The Incomplete Development of a Secular-Liberal Ethic

In 1948, Eleanor Roosevelt – chair of the human rights committee – commissioned a group of experts to draft the Universal Declaration of Human Rights (UDHR).[1] The group was led by the Canadian lawyer Chris Humphries, and their goal was to create a single document that would be accepted and applied by the multiple cultural traditions around the world. However, these traditions were based on significantly different worldviews and consequent social structures and behavioral norms. If the drafters attempted to construct an ideological synthesis, it would have been superficial at best. Thus, they did not seriously address the 'question of foundations'. That is, they did not fashion a theoretical basis that explained and legitimized the existence and substance of rights. Instead, they formed the document by accepting or rejecting particular articles based on relevance and applicability. Jacques Maritain – the French natural law representative – later explained the process by stating, "Men mutually opposed in their theoretical conceptions can come to a merely practical agreement regarding a list of human rights [based] on the condition that no one asks why."[2] Moreover, in the context of events such as World War II and the Holocaust, a document that appeared to lack a set of absolute principles must have seemed attractive and even necessary. This is because absolutism was used to justify many of the horrors witnessed by the twentieth century and the Universal Declaration was largely a response to those horrors:

---

[1] Although the UDHR was adopted as a declaration in 1948, its impact is virtually immeasurable. Grace Kao writes, "While the UDHR is only hortatory in character, it has inspired more than sixty human rights instruments and legally binding treaties…has arguably obtained the status of customary international law, and remains one of the most cited human rights documents today." See Grace Kao, *Grounding Human Rights in a Pluralist World* (Georgetown: Georgetown University Press, 2011), 173.

[2] Jacques Maritain, *Man and the State* (Washington, D.C.: The Catholic University of America Press, 1951), 76-77.

> Whereas disregard and contempt for human rights have resulted in barbarous acts which have outraged the conscience of mankind, and the advent of a world in which human beings shall enjoy freedom of speech and belief and freedom from fear and want has been proclaimed as the highest aspiration of the common people...[3]

Thus, the Universal Declaration was not created in an ideological vacuum. Although the drafters did not articulate any underlying principles, they existed in the form of an (incomplete) theory of secular-liberal rights derived from Christian natural law. Therefore, the Universal Declaration is clearly a product of its own history. Its culturally relative nature is largely responsible for the current backlash against international human rights in some parts of the world. It cuts the lines of cross-cultural communication and leads to calls of Western imperialism. This is because the Universal Declaration is steeped in the secular-liberal tradition and the latter's idealistic universalism seems to dismiss any divergent religious or philosophic approaches. In this regard, Abdulaziz Sachedina writes that,

> As long as the moral and metaphysical foundations of human rights norms remain unarticulated, they will be easily dismissed as yet another ploy to dominate Muslim societies by undermining their religiously based culture and value system. Moreover, ...Muslim authorities...have found it legitimate to dismiss compliance with some articles in the Universal Declaration...by labeling them as imperialistic or culturally Eurocentric, parallel with the "Asian Values" argument...[4]

For this reason, and in light of a newly emerging geopolitical order, it is necessary to consider a different approach. To this end, I begin this chapter by critically engaging popular human rights histories and their narrative that religion and human rights are alternative ideologies that present opposing paradigms of justice. More specifically, I challenge historical narratives that portray human rights – in its contemporary formulation – as humanity's 'saving' ideology. This critical engagement is necessary in order to 'open up a space of dialogue' and enable international human rights to adopt and operate within a paradigm of plurality. Recognizing multiple human rights models is the only way that human rights can become truly universal and

---

[3] "Universal Declaration of Human Rights," United Nations, accessed July 11, 2019, https://www.un.org/en/universal-declaration-human-rights/
[4] Abdulaziz Sachedina, *Islam and the Challenge of Human Rights* (New York: Oxford University Press, 2009), 5.

acceptable to the peoples of the world. Moreover, this recognition would carve out the desired middle position between universalism and cultural relativism. However, as mentioned, any overlapping consensus would be 'after-the-fact' and hence accidental as opposed to essential in nature. This type of consensus would ensure that a particular human rights paradigm is organic and integral to its own particular tradition, and not an artificial product that is planted based on an imagined Western moral superiority.

2.1. Popular human rights histories

The following is a summary proceeded by a critique of popular historical accounts about the development of human rights. This is important for two reasons. First, it provides the necessary context for the following chapter on human rights theory. Second, and more importantly, it is because historical sources play one of the most significant roles in producing contemporary attitudes towards human rights. These histories, along with human rights theory, need to be demystified before human rights can become truly universal.

It is possible to trace the concept of human rights back to the world's earliest known religions. For example, the Vedic scriptures and Judaic law both speak to social justice, human worth, and ethical conduct between individuals. The concept of human rights can also be traced back to earlier rational and secular philosophies. This is seen, for example, with Hammurabi (d.1750 B.C.E.) and his 'code of law'; Confucius (d.479 B.C.E.) and his vision of 'common humanity'; and Cyrus (d.530 B.C.E.) and his 'cylinder'.[5] However, these early religions and secular philosophies worked within the confines of hierarchical societies and focused on duties and moral responsibilities as opposed to personal-legal rights. Therefore, contemporary human rights – in its specific secular-liberal form – originated with the Renaissance and Protestant Reformation in the West. In this regard, Paul Lauren writes that

> The Renaissance of the fourteenth, fifteenth and sixteenth Centuries helped to spread ideas about the right to be free from censorship and intolerance by emphasizing human reason, individual expression, intellectual freedom and worldly experience… The Reformation and

---

[5] Human rights theorists often describe Confucius', Hammurabi's and Cyrus' thought and/or laws as secular. However, this view is highly questionable. For example, Hammurabi refers to his legal objectives using terms such as 'righteous', 'God-fearing', and 'evil-doers'. See "The Code of Hammurabi," tans. L. W. King, Yale Law School, The Avalon Project: Documents in Law, History and Diplomacy, accessed January 27, 2019, https://avalon.law.yale.edu/ancient/hamframe.asp

emergence of Protestantism in the fifteenth and sixteenth centuries…[emphasized] spiritual emancipation, individual conscience, freedom of religion and political and social reform. In doing so, all these forces combined to mark a shift in natural law, from (mainly religious) duties, to rights that were now understood to have a religious or secular basis.[6]

These ideas continued to be developed during the seventeenth century's so-called Age of Enlightenment. Most notably, Hugo Grotius (d.1645) – known as the father of international law – and John Locke (d.1704) – known as the father of modernism – argued that humans had natural rights and it was the government's duty to institute and protect them.[7] These ideas, along with the Habeas Corpus Act (1679) and the English Bill of Rights (1687), challenged the monarchy's claim to absolute rule. During the beginning of the eighteenth century, philosophers such as Montesquieu (d.1755), Voltaire (d.1778), and Rousseau (d.1778), continued to develop concepts that would eventually characterize the modern period: universalism, rationalism, empiricism, individualism and the like.[8] These ideas made up the philosophy of secular-humanism and the latter provided the ideological foundation for the newly established nation-states of America and France.[9] This is seen, for example, with the American adoption of The Declaration of Independence and the French institution of The Rights of Man and Citizen. Despite the highly universal language in these documents, however, many groups of people, such as women, slaves, and the poor, were excluded from the category 'human'. This changed, at least to some extent, in the nineteenth century, with the recognition of 'second-generation' rights, that is, social and economic

---

[6] Paul G. Lauren, "History of Human Rights," in *Encyclopedia of Human Rights*, ed. David P. Frosythe (New York: Oxford University Press, 2012), 396.

[7] Peter Laslett, ed., *Locke's Two Treatises of Government* (Cambridge: Cambridge University Press, 1988).

[8] For an overview of the philosophical idea of the times, see Anthony Kenny, *A New History of Western Philosophy* (Oxford: Oxford University Press, 2010).

[9] In the West, this turned modern societies into human rights societies in the same way that premodern societies were considered Christian. In other words, in the premodern West, the Church formed the foundation of society and Christian doctrine informed its societal institutions. However, the human rights revolution inverted this system. Human rights became the foundation of society and began to inform the latter's institutions, including the Church. This is can be seen in the rise of Protestantism, 'Christian human rights' and the Church's general goal of 'keeping up with the times'.

rights.[10] This was a by-product of the industrial revolution, which created poor working conditions that resulted in an exploited working class. Karl Marx (d.1883) and his followers argued in favor of revolution and the creation of a society free of private property and class struggle. Others opted to address the issue through the institution of labor unions and their concomitant mechanism of collective bargaining. Although the ideal of socialism was never fully realized, some human rights' historians, such as Micheline Ishay, recognize 'second-generation rights' as the socialist contribution to the global human rights movement.[11,12] In the twentieth century, the two World Wars largely determined – both in theory and practice – the development of international human rights. On the one hand, this period witnessed the violation of more rights than any other period in history. This was the result of a combination of factors: colonialism; the Great Depression; the rise of nationalism; the regimes of Mussolini (d.1945), Stalin (d.1953), and Hitler (d.1945); and perhaps most significantly, the civilian casualties of World War II. On the other hand, this period also destroyed old power structures; a space was created for the establishment of new institutions based on personal-legal rights. Moreover, groups that were previously excluded from having human rights, such as women and slaves, contributed to the war campaign, and on the basis of their contributions they demanded to have their rights recognized. Among other changes, this resulted in the recognition of 'third-generation' rights, that is, collective or group rights. Thus, by the end of the twentieth century, for example, women had the right to vote, and nation-states were afforded the right to self-determination – at least in theory and to some degree. Moreover, the horrors of World War II and the Holocaust evoked the 'conscience of mankind', and they led to the establishment of the United Nations and the drafting of the Universal Declaration of Human Rights. Eleanor Roosevelt assembled a group of experts that represented a wide range of religious and cultural values; they deliberated and debated on a number of

---

[10] These are also known as 'freedom-to' or positive rights as opposed to 'freedom-from' or negative rights.
[11] Micheline R. Ishay, *The History of Human Rights: From Ancient Times to the Globalization Era* (Berkeley: University of California Press, 2004), 4.
[12] The problem with this view is that it seems to ignore the fact that neo-Marxists generally understand human rights as an oppressive ideology that is implemented and used by the economic elite to further their own agendas. In this regard, see Leszek Kolakowski, "Marxism and Human Rights," *The MIT Press* 112, no. 4 (1983): 81-92.

human rights' issues until they reached a consensus of sorts.[13] The National Assembly passed the Universal Declaration in 1948 and thus began the new world order of international human rights. This brief historical overview is typical of popular accounts concerning the history of human rights.[14]

2.2. The construction and assumptions of human rights histories

These types of histories generally share some, if not all, of the following assumptions. First, they see the development of human rights as linear and progressive. In this sense, they perpetuate one of the dominant ideologies of the Enlightenment period. Immanuel Kant (d.1804) aptly summarized this view on progress when he wrote that

> The history of mankind can be seen, in the large, as the realization of Nature's secret plan to bring forth a perfectly constituted state as the only condition in which the capacities of mankind can be fully developed, and also bring forth that external relation among states which is perfectly adequate to this end.[15]

This idea of progress is not always explicitly laid out in contemporary human rights narratives. This seems to be the case because the ideology is becoming increasingly contentious. In other words, the ideology of progress is being re-examined and questioned in light of current world affairs, such as the global environmental crisis. It is also being examined in light of postmodern thought and its deconstruction of linear-progressive ideologies.[16] Nevertheless, the theme is almost always discernible in some form and to some degree. For example, Lauren writes that the history of human rights did not have a straight line of development and sometimes regression was paradoxically needed as a springboard for progress.[17] According to Ishay:

---

[13] However, this 'representation' was incomplete because it excluded significant segments of the world's population. Moreover, the drafters' agreement was exclusively practical with little to no agreement on any fundamental issues.

[14] For example, see: Ishay, *History of Human Rights* and Lauren, "History of Human Rights."

[15] Immanuel Kant, "Idea for a Universal History from a Cosmopolitan Point of View," Marxist Internet Archive, accessed December 15, 2017, https://www.marxists.org/reference/subject/ethics/kant/universal-history.htm.

[16] In general, see Stuart Sim, ed., *The Routledge Companion to Postmodernism*, 2nd ed. (New York: Routledge, 2005).

[17] Lauren, "History of Human Rights," 394.

That is not to say that reactionary forces have completely nullified each phase of progress in human rights. Rather, history preserves the human rights record as each generation builds on the hopes and achievements of its predecessors while struggling to free itself from authoritarianism and improve its social conditions.[18]

Even Lynn Hunt's *Inventing Human Rights*, which describes the 'trial and error' nature behind the development of rights, gives the impression that the latter developed according to its own inherent, albeit unpredictable, progressive nature.[19] It can be argued that this belief in progress developed in light of the scientific and industrial revolutions in the West; these revolutions gave people the impression that humans possessed an unlimited potential for discovery and development. Moreover, in light of increased scientific knowledge and a higher standard of living, people generally began to believe that these modern developments were positive and, therefore, they should be pursued by all means and without end. Today however, many experts, particularly in the fields of science and philosophy, are questioning how much we actually know about the world, and even if there is such a thing as objective knowledge at all. Furthermore, changes in science, industry, and technology have seemingly alienated human beings and created the setting needed for a large-scale existential crisis. Hence, it is this existential angst that is partially responsible for the rise of mass consumerism and the contemporary growth of numerous new-age spiritual movements. In this light, 'progress' has come at a cost, and this cost arguably means that there has been no actual progress at all. In other words, it can be argued that scientific and material progress have also caused individual and spiritual regress; therefore, the notion of holistic and collective progress over time cannot be taken as a matter of fact. In any case, in relation to human rights, Samuel Moyn argues that these 'celebratory histories' are religious in nature because they interpret every setback as a necessary stage in 'furthering the cause'. He maintains that history has always allowed for a number of open possibilities; therefore, human rights should not be seen as the inevitable, saving-truth of humankind.[20] In this regard, Moyn writes that

---

[18] Ishay, *The History of Human Rights*, 4.
[19] See Lyn Hunt, *Inventing Human Rights: A History* (New York: W.W. Norton and Company, 2008).
[20] See Samuel Moyn, *The Last Utopia: Human Rights in History* (London: Harvard University Press, 2010).

> In recasting world history as raw material for the progressive ascent of international human rights, [contemporary historians] have rarely conceded that earlier history left open diverse paths into the future, rather than paving a single road toward current ways of thinking and acting...historians have been loath to regard [human rights] as only one appealing ideology among others. Instead, they have used history to confirm their inevitable rise...A different approach is needed to reveal the true origins of this most recent utopian program.[21]

The second assumption of popular human rights' histories is that they generally consider the world's earliest known religions as an important historical stage in the history of human rights. For example, Ishay begins her book on human rights with a section on world religions. She states that "religions contain the humanistic elements that anticipated our modern conception of rights." [22] In a similar fashion, Lauren writes that "...some of the first significant philosophies...would come from religious traditions...whose principles would inform later human rights developments."[23] Thus, these histories locate proto-human rights concepts in selected passages of sacred scripture dealing with the themes of justice and morality.[24] After connecting religion and human rights, however, these historians generally proceed to sever the connection with the rise of the Renaissance and Protestant Reformation. At this point, religion becomes 'stagnant' and 'backwards', and the newly born concept of secular-liberal human rights begins to develop. Interestingly, they argue that religion was partially responsible for the birth of human rights, but now, the two approaches are largely irreconcilable. In this regard, Thomas Banchoff and Robert Wuthrow write:

> It is common for writers to argue that the modern conception of human rights triumphed only as traditional religious authorities eroded... The story usually makes some acknowledgement [of religious contributions] ... But the dominant story is one of traditional religious authority opposed to the secular Enlightenment ideal of rational, autonomous individuals as bearers of universal rights... In this view it is legitimate for religious people to insist on freedom of belief and

---

[21] Moyn, *Last Utopia*, 5.
[22] Ishay, *History of Human Rights*, 5.
[23] Lauren, "History of Human Rights," 395.
[24] They also locate them in earlier rational and secular philosophies. However, as mentioned, the claim that these philosophies are secular in nature is dubious at best.

worship. But when they join with others of like mind about different policy agendas, they should do so as citizens and not as people of faith. To engage more broadly in the politics of human rights – to press their own ideas of what those rights mean and how they grow out of their traditions – is to inject religion where it does not belong…[25]

This view concerning the connection between religion and human rights is contested on two fronts. First, it is contested by human rights advocates that argue that 'religion as a historical stage' is misleading because there is no interdependence between the two ideologies. For example, Donnelly argues that religions did not have a word for 'subjective right', that is, a word that referred to individual rights. Instead, they exclusively focused on 'objective rights', that is, on the idea of 'what is right/good'. In other words, Donnelly distinguishes between 'it is right that' and 'the right to', and he argues that the latter exclusively came into existence with modern political theory. Therefore, according to Donnelly, human rights are exclusively Western and modern.[26,27] However, the view of 'religion as a historical stage' is also contested by human rights proponents that argue that the Renaissance and Enlightenment periods did not produce 'new ideas' that formed the foundation of all subsequent human rights developments. For these theorists, human rights are a perennial issue that have always existed in the world's religious traditions.[28] For example, Bonny Ibhawoh mentions that pre-colonial African societies had a concept of justice that was informed by rights and supported a measure of individualism.[29] Therefore, according to this view, human rights are not exclusive to the Western liberal tradition or only relevant in reference to post-1948 developments.

---

[25] Thomas Banchoff and Robert Wuthrow, "Introduction," in *Religion and the Global Politics of Human Rights*, ed. Thomas Banchoff and Robert Wuthrow (New York: Oxford University Press. 2011), 4.

[26] Jack Donnelly, "Human Rights and Human Dignity: An Analytic critique of Non-Western Conceptions of Human Rights," *The American Political Science Review* 76, no. 2 (1982): 303-16.

[27] For a critique of this position, see Michael Freeman, "Beyond Capitalism and Socialism," in *Human Rights and Capitalism: A Multidisciplinary Perspective on Globalisation*, ed. Janet Dine and Andrew Fagan (Edward Algar Publishing, 2006), 8-9.

[28] On the continuous intersection between religion and human rights, see Banchoff and Wuthrow, "Introduction," 1-22.

[29] Bonny Ibhawoh, "Restraining Universalism: Africanist Perspectives on Cultural Relativism in the Human Rights Discourse," in *Human Rights, The Rule of Law and Development in Africa*, ed. Paul T. Zeleza and Philip J. McConnaughy (Philadelphia: University of Pennsylvania Press, 2004), 21-39.

The last common assumption is that the Medieval Age was a 'dark' and oppressive time in the Western world. This period is generally painted as being full of disease, poverty, and enslavement. It is remembered as a time of stark class distinction – from kings down to peasants. Although this depiction is partially true, the Medieval Age covers a long period of history (approximately 476 -1500 C.E.), and, therefore, it cannot be generalized in one single way. According to Norman Cantor, along with oft-mentioned events such as the inquisition, this period also saw times of unprecedented creativity and growth that was due to, and not despite of, the church and ruling aristocratic system.[30] Martin Lings also challenges this dominant assumption and counter-intuitively argues that the Middle Ages would have been even 'darker' if it had not been for the church and the prevailing social structure.[31] Finally, Nasr argues that premodern Christians in the Western world had a profound sense of meaning and purpose – a sense that is missing today. For him, this purpose and meaning outweighed any external problems that existed before the Renaissance. In this light, he writes:

> Human beings are in need of meaning as much as they are in need of air to breathe and food to eat. Modern materialistic reductionism has not only resulted in chemically infested food and polluted air, but also the loss of meaning in its ultimate sense. There can in fact be no ultimate meaning without the acceptance of the Ultimate in the metaphysical sense. It is indeed a great paradox that human consciousness in modern times has produced a view of the cosmos which has no room for consciousness. And when human beings do seek to find consciousness in the objective world, or experience what they consider to be encounters with conscious beings outside of the human realm, they are marginalized and condemned to the category of hallucinating men and women in need of psychiatric care.[32]

Critically challenging popular historical accounts is important because they play a central role in determining the attitudes and practices related to international human rights today. For example, the belief in progress – culminating in the establishment of a universal human rights regime – justifies an 'us/them' mentality, and it is closely related to the dubious

---

[30] Norman F. Cantor, *Inventing the Middle Ages* (New York: Harper, 1991), 17-47.
[31] Martin Lings, *Ancient Beliefs and Modern Superstitions* (Cambridge: Archetype Chetwynd House, 2001), 48.
[32] William C. Chittick, ed., *The Essential Seyyed Hossein Nasr* (Indiana: World Wisdom, 2010), 227.

practice of humanitarian intervention. Moreover, these histories tend to demonize, undermine, and/or misunderstand other belief systems and their various manifestations. My argument, therefore, is simple: popular human rights histories unfairly approach religion and function as an impediment to dialogue and, ultimately, positive social change.

In the next chapter, I critically examine some of the different theories that attempt to provide a rationale for the existence and implementation of universal human rights norms. I argue that these theories are problematic, and that it is this lack of justification that is one of the greatest obstacles to the international implementation of human rights. I then proceed to conclude the chapter by briefly discussing some of the human rights views coming out of the African, Asian, and Islamic traditions.

Chapter 3

Human Rights and Their Underlying Ethical Theories

The American Declaration of Independence (1776) and the French Rights of Man and Citizen (1789) both claim that human rights are self-evident. Thomas Jefferson famously wrote: "We hold these truths to be self-evident, that all men are created equal, that they are endowed by their Creator with certain unalienable Rights, that among these are Life, Liberty and the pursuit of Happiness."[1] However, there is ambiguity and disagreement on virtually every human rights issue, including that of their existence as a whole. Alasdair McIntyre goes as far as to say that "there are no such rights, and belief in them is one with belief in witches and unicorns."[2] Thus, the argument of 'self-evidence' is insufficient; human rights need to be justified. On what *basis* do human beings have universal, equal, and inalienable rights? If this question remains unanswered, the implementation of international human rights will be virtually impossible. The following chapter critically engages some of the popular ethical theories that are used in an attempt to answer the question of foundations.[3] More specifically, I critically explore the theories of utilitarianism, natural rights, and ethical sentimentalism. This leads me to argue that each of these ideologies is deeply problematic and vulnerable to objections of relativism. Therefore, the aggressive implementation of human rights based on any one of these theories is arbitrary and a form of cultural imperialism. Moreover, it is important to note that this chapter exclusively focuses on ethical theories within the secular-liberal tradition. This is in order to underscore the undeniable fact that there is no good reason to close off alternative human rights visions originating from other cultural traditions. Thus, this chapter paves the way for the construction of an Islamic theory of

---

[1] "The Declaration of Independence," US History, accessed July 4, 2019, https://www.ushistory.org/declaration/document/
[2] Alasdair MacIntyre, *After Virtue: A Study in Moral Theory*, 3rd ed. (Indiana: University of Notre Dame Press, 2007), 69.
[3] This section is not intended to be comprehensive; therefore, it leaves out theories that are less common or persuasive. Moreover, its discussion of Islam as a source of human rights is purposefully brief since it treats the subject in the following chapters.

virtue ethics which has the ability to 'ground' a vision of human rights based on the Islamic intellectual tradition.

3.1. A critical exploration of utilitarianism

Utilitarianism is a consequentialist political and moral philosophy. It argues that actions are morally good or bad depending on the consequences they produce. For act-based utilitarians, this normative moral principle should be applied on a case-by-case basis. For example, an act-based utilitarian would maintain that in some scenarios, taking a person's life is the right course of action, while in other scenarios, taking a person's life is the wrong course of action. It depends on the situation. For rule-based utilitarians, however, this normative principle should be applied to establish general rules that produce the greatest amount of utility. For example, a rule-based utilitarian would maintain that taking someone's life generally produces more negative consequences than positive ones; therefore, it is the wrong course of action as a rule.[4] There are many variations within these two strands of utilitarianism; however, they all agree that actions are intrinsically valueless; their morality depends on the consequences they produce. This is in stark contrast to deontological natural rights theory in both its religious and secular forms. Many early ideas concerning utilitarianism came from Christian theologians, such as Richard Cumberland (d.1718) and John Gay (d.1745), who believed that promoting happiness was an imperative by God and that morally correct behavior would always achieve this end.[5] However, the classical and formal exposition of utilitarianism is normally traced back to Jeremy Bentham (d.1832). According to him,

> Nature has placed mankind under the governance of two sovereign masters, *pain* and *pleasure*. It is for them alone to point out what we ought to do, as well as to determine what we shall do. On the one hand the standard of right and wrong, on the other the chain of causes and effects, are fastened to their throne. They govern us in all we do, in all we say, in all we think: every effort we can make to throw off our subjection, will serve but to demonstrate and confirm it. In words a

---

[4] In general, see Stephen Nathanson, "Act and Rule Utilitarianism," Internet Encyclopedia of Philosophy: A Peer-Reviewed Academic Resource, accessed March 13, 2017, https://www.iep.utm.edu/util-a-r/.

[5] In general, see Julia Driver, "The History of Utilitarianism," The Stanford Encyclopedia of Philosophy, accessed January 2, 2017, https://plato.stanford.edu/entries/utilitarianism-history/.

man may pretend to abjure their empire: but in reality he will remain subject to it all the while. The *principle of utility* recognizes this subjection, and assumes it for the foundation of that system, the object of which is to rear the fabric of felicity by the hands of reason and of law. Systems which attempt to question it, deal in sounds instead of sense, in caprice instead of reason, in darkness instead of light.[6]

According to Bentham then, individual behavior, along with governmental laws and policies, should be based on the attempt to maximize the greatest amount of happiness for the greatest number of people. This view of 'utility as happiness or pleasure' is commonly referred to as hedonistic utilitarianism. John Stuart Mill (d.1873) – following in Bentham's footsteps – refined the theory to address a number of problems.[7] The difference between the two concerned their understanding of the human being and the nature of pleasure. Mill argued that people intuitively and experientially know that some kinds of acts are more pleasurable and fitting than others. For example, he argued that there was a significant qualitative difference between sensual pleasures and intellectual pleasures. Thus, according to Mill,

> It is indisputable that the being whose capacities of enjoyment are low, has the greatest chance of having them fully satisfied; and a highly endowed being will always feel that any happiness which he can look for, as the world is constituted, is imperfect. But he can learn to bear its imperfections…It is better to be a human being dissatisfied than a pig satisfied; better to be Socrates dissatisfied than a fool satisfied. And if the fool, or the pig, is of a different opinion, it is only because they only know their own side of the question.[8]

Another important distinction between Bentham and Mill was that the latter placed more emphasis on the importance of treating one's 'neighbor' well. Keeping in line with hedonism, Mill argued that harming others causes pain to oneself while helping others causes pleasure to oneself. Therefore, Mill's adaptive hedonism opened the door to utilitarianism's subsequent connection to human rights. This is because it argued that it is in the collective self-interest to protect and promote the rights of others. Despite

---

[6] Jeremy Bentham, "An Introduction to the Principles and Morals of Legislation," Library of Economics and Liberty, accessed March 2, 2017, https://www.econlib.org/library/Bentham/bnthPML.html?chapter_num=19#book-reader.
[7] See John Stuart Mill, *Utilitarianism*, ed. T. N. R. Rogers (Dover Publications, 2007).
[8] Mill, *Utilitarianism*, 8.

Mill's best efforts, however, hedonistic utilitarianism was heavily criticized. One of the most decisive critiques came from Robert Nozick (d.2002) and his 'experience machine' thought experiment.[9] Nozick asked his readers to think of a machine that could induce the highest feelings of pleasure. If hedonistic utilitarians were correct, then everyone would choose to spend their lives drugged in the machine. However, Nozick argued that most people would not enter the 'experience machine', and that they would consider it a waste of life. His point was simple: people value many different types of human experiences.[10] For example, Nozick's thought experiment suggests that some people may consider the experience of reality more valuable than the experience of happiness. After Bentham and Mill, a number of theorists attempted to expand utilitarianism in order to include a wider range of human experiences. For example, George Edward Moore (d.1958) wrote in favor of an ideal utilitarianism based on intuition.[11] Moore was an ontological realist and argued that we cannot know *how* we know things; however, this does not mean that we cannot know things. His ontological realism extended to his theory of morality. According to Moore, 'goodness' is a real property that we can know through our common sense. Moreover, it can be attached to any number of objects or state of affairs, and these can be ranked according to their degree of 'goodness'. Hence, according to Moore, an ideal state is one that is good in itself and good to a high degree. Therefore, ideal utilitarianism is a moral theory in which "actions are to be ordered not to the greatest happiness or pleasure, but to those state of affairs possessing the highest degree of good."[12] However, as I later argue in this chapter, Moore's theory does not escape the seemingly inherent problems in all forms of utilitarianism. The same can be said of contemporary utilitarian theories. According to Will Kymlicka, these contemporary theories can be categorized into four broad groups: hedonistic utility, non-hedonistic mental-state utility,

---

[9] This critique was already popular during Mill's time; however, Nozick's 'experience machine' was significant in its powerful imagery and incisive critique.

[10] Dale Murray, "Robert Nozick: Political Philosophy," Internet Encyclopedia of Philosophy: A Peer-Reviewed Academic Resource, accessed March 29, 2017, https://www.iep.utm.edu/noz-poli/.

[11] For an overview, see Thomas Baldwin, ed., *G. E. Moore: Selected Writings* (London: Routledge, 1993).

[12] Aaron Preston, "George Edward Moore (1873-1958)," Internet Encyclopedia of Philosophy: A Peer-Reviewed Academic Resource, accessed January 22, 2017, https://www.iep.utm.edu/moore/.

preference satisfaction and informed preferences.[13] To provide one example, R. M. Hare's (d.2002) theory of 'universal prescriptivism' argues in favor of utilitarianism based on 'informed preferences'.[14] According to him, laws should be created in light of overall human welfare and that the latter should be judged according to the satisfaction of informed and rational human preferences. In explaining Hare's stance, Anthony Price writes:

> In their practical force, ideals are equivalent to universal preferences that differ from personal preferences in their content, but owe their moral weight to the prevalence and intensity of whatever preferences their realization would satisfy... The emergent ethical theory is a distinctive variety of utilitarianism, one that identifies the moral good with the maximization not of some subjective state such as happiness, but of the satisfaction of preferences.[15]

Closely related to utilitarianism's 'informed preferences' is Amartya Sen's popular capabilities theory.[16] According to Sen, the problem with utilitarianism is its lack of attention to the 'morality of means'. In other words, the problem is that it doesn't evaluate the morality of the process by which a good or bad consequence is produced. Thus, Sen argues for a kind of 'comprehensive utilitarianism'. For him, a person's capability represents "the effective freedom of an individual to choose between different functioning combinations – between different kinds of life – that she has reason to value."[17] Thus, one of Sen's underlying concerns is not only to evaluate the means that people have access to, but to also evaluate the specific capabilities, that is, 'functioning combinations', that people have to use those means. For example, the human right to the 'freedom of movement' is insufficient if a particular person is handicapped and, therefore, unable to move.

---

[13] An in-depth study of utilitarianism is beyond the scope of this work. For a more detailed overview of utilitarianism see Will Kymlicka, *Contemporary Political Philosophy: An Introduction*, 2nd ed. (Oxford: Oxford University Press, 2002), 10-53.

[14] R. M. Hare, *Moral Thinking: Its Levels, Method and Point* (Oxford: Oxford University Press, 1993).

[15] Anthony Price, "Richard Mervyn Hare," The Stanford Encyclopedia of Philosophy, accessed September 9, 2017, https://plato.stanford.edu/entries/hare/.

[16] In general, see Amartya Sen, *Commodities and Capabilities* (Oxford: Oxford University Press, 1999).

[17] Thomas Wells, "Sen's Capability Approach," Internet Encyclopedia of Philosophy: A Peer-Reviewed Academic Resource, accessed March 24, 2019, https://www.iep.utm.edu/sen-cap/.

Contemporary utilitarianism is an extremely appealing moral theory because it is consequentialist; therefore, it provides moral objectivity through practical calculation. This means that it has the potential to ground rights in absolute values without having to appeal to God or any other transcendent entity. Simply put, something is moral if it provides utility and immoral if it doesn't. However, all forms of utilitarianism – from 'hedonistic' to 'informed preferences' – face at least two seemingly insurmountable problems, and these two problems rightly question utilitarianism's ability to 'ground' human rights. First, utilitarianism, by definition, sacrifices the individual – whenever necessary – for the sake of society at large, that is, for the sake of the greater good. This is obviously antithetical to the concept of individual rights. In this regard, Jermome Shestack writes that,

> Despite the egalitarian pretensions of utilitarian doctrine, it has a sinister side in which the well-being of the individual may be sacrificed for what are claimed to be aggregate interests, and justice and right have no secure place. Utilitarian philosophy thus leave liberty and rights vulnerable to contingencies, and therefore at risk[18]

However, the argument of 'utilitarian sacrifice' does not unequivocally dismiss the theory as a possible justification for human rights. This is because rights are always clashing in practice and, therefore, utilitarian calculations are unavoidable. Andrew Heard correctly observes that

> ...Resources are scarce in any society, and especially limited in some. This scarcity inevitably leads to utilitarian calculation to allocate those resources in a way that will maximize the greatest good. In the end, it is argued, all the benefits listed as human rights, even life itself, are subject to the promotion of the greatest good within society. As such an individual's benefits claims as a human right may be compromised, diluted or even completely denied in specific situations where that right has to be weighed against the claim of another individual or society as a whole.[19]

---

[18] Jerome J. Shestack, "The Philosophical Foundations of Human Rights," in *Exploring International Human Rights*, ed. Rhonda L. Callaway and Julie Harrelson-Stephens (London: Lynne Rienner Pub., 2007), 26.

[19] Andrew Heard, "The Challenges of Utilitarianism and Relativism," Simon Fraser University, accessed January 6, 2019, http://www.sfu.ca/~aheard/417/util.html.

Hence, it is really the second argument that undermines utilitarianism as a 'ground' for human rights. This argument is based on 'the problem of relativity' and can be broken down into three interrelated parts: First, utilitarian calculations assume that it is possible to know all the different effects that a particular act or rule will produce. However, people's knowledge of effects is obviously limited; therefore, there is no way to unequivocally justify one choice over another. To provide an obvious example, in some secular societies, one's sexuality falls within the private sphere; a person's sexual actions are a matter of the right to freedom and individual choice. However, these supposedly private acts can have great public ramifications. Infidelity often leads to broken homes which are strongly correlated with drug abuse, criminality, and the like. Second, a single human rights theory based on utilitarianism is forced to make the assumption that human choices are the same with individuals and across communities. However, 'human utility' is relative to a person's or community's particular worldview and consequent understanding of the purpose of life. To provide another obvious example, a practicing religious person would undoubtedly understand their highest goal as related to salvation; therefore, their understanding would clash with various secular opinions concerning the 'the good'. Finally, putting aside the first two problems, utilitarianism is still left with the problem of qualitative measurement. Even if all people and societies agreed on 'the good', it would still be impossible to precisely measure and determine what produces more or less utility. Thus, the claim that a universal standard of morality can be known by measuring the consequences of common acts or rules is highly problematic, and it cannot ground human rights in a way that allows the latter to be universal, equal, and inalienable.

3.2. A critical exploration of natural rights

Natural rights theory is the liberal response to utilitarianism. Its religious version can be traced back to Christian natural law and its classical representative – saint Thomas Aquinas (d.1274). Aquinas argued that God governs the world through Divine Reason; consequently, all creatures obey an 'Eternal Law'. This is because they are given particular natures that incline them to act in a particular way. However, according to Aquinas, human beings are special because they possess free will and the choice to follow their God-given essence. In order to guide their free will, God gave humans a share in his Divine Reason; therefore, they have the ability to discern between good (legal) from evil (illegal).[20] Aquinas wrote that

---

[20] Clarence Morris, ed., *The Great Legal Philosophers. Selected Readings in Jurisprudence* (Pennsylvania: University of Pennsylvania Press, 1959), 56-79.

> Among all others, the rational creature is subject to Divine Providence in the most excellent way, in so far as it partakes of a share of providence, by being provident both for itself, and for others. Wherefore, it has a share of the Eternal Reason, whereby it has a natural inclination to its proper act and end.[21]

Natural rights theory picked up on the concept that human beings are 'special' and, therefore, 'naturally' entitled to individual rights. Grounding these rights in a transcendent God gave the former a universal and ahistorical character; it legitimized the claim that human rights are held by all human beings irrespective of class, race, or gender. However, the traditional concept of God did not sit well with the Enlightenment's program of secular-liberalism.[22] That is, it did not sit well with its program of lifting reason above revelation and constructing a worldview based on science rather than tradition. In the words of Kant, the Enlightenment was a process that involved "man's release from his self-incurred immaturity."[23] Thus, Christian natural law needed to be modified. Philosophers such as Voltaire (d.1778) and Diderot (d.1784) decided to sever the 'Church's God' from reason and nature. They believed that the latter two could still provide the necessary metaphysical foundation for ethics since they – like God – seemed to operate beyond the confines of space and time. It was this change that gave birth to a number of modern natural right theories within the secular-liberal ethical tradition.[24]

Modern natural rights theory is normally traced back to John Locke and his imaginative state of nature. According to Locke, all people in a state of nature would be considered equal and free; however, they would also lack protection and security from others. Hence, according to Locke's thought experiment, free and equal people would come together and decide to create a social

---

[21] Morris, *Great Legal Philosophers*, 61.

[22] The Enlightenment was a complex historical period that was driven by diverse voices which varied within and across geographical locations. In this regard, see Dorinda Outram, *The Enlightenment*, 2nd ed. (Cambridge: Cambridge University Press, 2005). Nevertheless, the Enlightenment's basic program is generally understood as a movement away from traditional authority towards individual autonomy.

[23] As quoted in: Outram, *The Enlightenment*, 1.

[24] Sachedina argues that this change is largely responsible for the friction between secular-liberal human rights and other religious and philosophic approaches. Thus, he argues for a return to Christian natural rights and claims that the latter can work with Islamic natural law theories to provide the principles necessary for universal human rights. See Sachedina, *Islam and the Challenge*. Also see Enver M. Emon, *Islamic Natural Law Theories* (Oxford, Oxford University Press, 2010).

contract. This contract would establish a government invested with political authority and the responsibility to protect people. More specifically, its responsibility would be to protect what belonged to people by right of birth; namely, their right to life, liberty, and property. Furthermore, the same people could rightfully rebel against the government if it failed in fulfilling its existential function.[25] Thus, Locke assumed that human rights were grounded in a universal human nature, and that the government acted as a 'Law-Enforcer' to protect those rights. In his second treatise, Locke wrote:

> To understand Political Power right…we must consider what State all Men are naturally in, and that is, a *State of perfect Freedom* to order their Actions, and dispose of their Possessions, and Persons as they think fit, within the bounds of the Law of Nature, without asking leave, or depending upon the Will of any other Man.[26]

Moreover, he continued:

> And that all Men may be restrained from invading others Rights, and from doing hurt to one another, and the Law of Nature be observed, which willeth the Peace and *Preservation of all Mankind*, the *Execution* of the Law of Nature is in that State, put into every Mans hands… For the *Law of Nature* would, as all other Laws that concern Men in this World, be in vain, if there were no body that in the State of Nature, had a P*ower to Execute* that Law, and thereby preserve the innocent and restrain offenders…[27]

Immanuel Kant also developed a highly influential secular natural rights theory. His goal was to discover a 'metaphysics of morality', that is, a set of *a priori* moral principles that could be applied universally. He did this by developing a theory of 'transcendental idealism' that distinguished between the world of phenomena (appearances) and noumena (reality).[28] According to Kant, human beings cannot know the world as it is; they can only access it through concepts such as cause and effect. However, according to Kant, these

---

[25] Alex Tuckness, "Locke's Political Philosophy," The Stanford Encyclopedia of Philosophy, accessed September 30, 2017, https://plato.stanford.edu/entries/locke-political/.
[26] Laslett, ed., *Locke's Two Treatises*, 91.
[27] Laslett, ed., *Locke's Two Treatises*, 92.
[28] In general, see: Immanuel Kant, *Grounding for the Metaphysics of Morals*, 3rd ed, trans. James W. Ellington (Indianapolis: Hackett, 1993).

mental concepts are universal and naturally embedded in every rational mind. Hence, Kant restricted his search for a moral imperative to the rational sphere. He maintained that the principle would have to be an 'end in and of itself' and a moral obligation on all rational agents. Kant discovered this principle in his famous categorical imperative: "Act only according to that maxim whereby you can at the same time will that it should become a universal law."[29] This, he believed, provided the litmus test for ethical action, and that it could be further developed and applied in all moral contexts.

It was the concept of natural rights based on nature and/or reason that became the theoretical force behind the French and American revolutions. Locke's work was widely disseminated among the people; it justified rebellion and the establishment of a government that was "of the people, by the people, and for the people." Eventually, natural law theory, as articulated by philosophers such as Locke and Kant, also became the doctrinal basis for modern societies grounded in some form of secular-liberalism. This was despite the fact that their ideas were never fully developed and heavily criticized. It was also despite the fact that many members of these societies opposed the social changes that accompanied this doctrinal shift.[30] Moreover, the Universal Declaration was drafted within the context of this momentous change; hence, it was underpinned by the same incomplete neo-lockean principles. Despite these problems, however, the strengths of natural rights theories could not be ignored; thus, it was picked up by contemporary human rights theorists, such as John Rawls (d.2002), John Finnis (d.1980) and David Gauthier (d.1986). In their own ways, they attempted to use natural rights theory to ground human rights so that the latter could be considered universal, equal, and inalienable. For example, Rawls carried out a thought experiment in which people were placed in an 'original position' of sorts; however, instead of the classic 'state of nature', Rawls used what he referred to as the 'veil of ignorance'.[31] Behind the veil, people are denied any knowledge of who they are; they have no way of knowing their gender, race, and socio-economic status. It is based on this ignorance, and its assumed impartiality, that people must decide what principles constitute a just society. Rawls argued that rational people would choose a 'politically liberal' society, one where justice is based on fairness and constitutes two principles:

---

[29] Kant, *Grounding*, 30.
[30] In this regard, see Hunt, *Inventing Human Rights*.
[31] See Rawls, *A Theory of Justice*, 118-94.

> The first principle states that each person in a society is to have as much basic liberty as possible, as long as everyone is granted the same liberties… The second principle states that while social and economic inequalities can be just, they must be available to everyone equally (that is, no one is to be on principle denied access to greater economic advantage) and such inequalities must be to the advantage of everyone.[32]

Finnis, on the other hand, developed a theory of 'neo-naturalism' that attempted to move away from the classical appeals to God, reason, and nature. Instead, he argued that human rights should be grounded in the concept of objective goods, that is, goods that are necessary for human flourishing. Interestingly however, this change brought Finnis' ideas closer to utilitarianism than to natural rights. This is because his idea concerning 'necessary goods' required a social consensus about which 'goods' are more valuable than others based on (impossible) calculations of their qualitative values. In this way, many neo-natural rights theories have lost their classical appeal, that is, the appeal of a human rights model grounded in a transcendent and objective source. In any case, despite the strengths of natural rights theories, they all seem to face the same two-fold problem of universal consensus and practical application. For example, in terms of universality, Locke's idea that life, liberty, and property are natural, equal, and inalienable seems to be heavily influenced by the absolutism of the seventeenth and eighteenth centuries. Carrying out the same thought experiment in different social contexts would produce different sets of rights, and the latter could just as easily be considered natural, equal, and inalienable. Moreover, in terms of application, the rights to life, liberty, and property are general concepts. Even if people agreed on the substance of basic rights, they would undoubtedly disagree on the ways in which these rights should interact with each other and with other rights when put into practice. Critiques of contemporary natural rights theories point to these two problems. For example, Alison Rentln argues that natural human rights are wrongly considered universal because people have a psychological predisposition to generalize from their own particular perspectives; they have a tendency to project their moral categories onto others. In arguing this point in relation to Rawls, she writes,

---

[32] Celeste Friend, "Social Contract Theory," Internet Encyclopedia of Philosophy: A Peer-Reviewed Academic Resource, accessed April 22, 2017, https://www.iep.utm.edu/soc-cont/#:~:text=Rousseau's%20social%20contract%20theories%20together,by%20our%20contingent%20social%20history.

> It is plausible that individuals from the same culture might agree to the same principles...But if one transposes the scenario of the original position to an international setting, it becomes doubtful whether all the participants will acquiesce. The presupposition is that individuals stripped of their cultural and political heritage would be pure rational being and would thus dutifully elect liberal democratic principles of justice. The premise that individuals could negotiate for fundamental principles in the absence of culture is quite fantastic. And this is precisely the root of the problem: underlying the presumption of universality is the belief that all peoples think in a similar fashion.[33]

Similarly, in the case of Finnis' objective goods theory, Michael Freeman writes, "claims about objective goods are either too vague to be useful or too controversial to be objective. Even those who agree there are objective goods do not agree on what those goods are."[34]. Thus, it seems that that the movement away from a transcendent God was a movement towards relativity and the loss of universality. Despite this, however, some human rights theorists, such as Johannes Morsink, argue that the Universal Declaration cannot be criticized on the same grounds because it decidedly distanced itself from the secular-liberal conception of natural rights.[35] However, according to critics of 'universal' human rights, this view is deeply problematic since The Declaration's separation from Western liberal values was clearly incomplete. For example, Prakash Sinha's study shows how the Western concept of social order that underpins human rights is not shared by non-Western civilizations. According to Sinha,

> There are three basic tenets that are inherent in the present formulation of human rights. One, the fundamental unit of society is the individual, not the family. Two, the primary basis for securing human existence in society is through rights, not duties. Three, the primary method of securing these rights is through reconciliation...not legalism.[36]

---

[33] Alison D. Renteln, "The Concept of Human Rights," *Anthropos Institute* 83, no. 4 (1988): 349.

[34] Michael Freeman, *Human Rights: An Interdisciplinary Approach* (Cambridge: Polity Press), 70.

[35] Johannes Morsink, *The Universal Declaration of Human Rights: Origins, Drafting and Intent* (Pennsylvania: University of Pennsylvania Press, 1999).

[36] Prakash Sinha, "Human Rights: A Non-Western Viewpoint," *Archives for Philosophy of Law and Social Philosophy* 67, no. 1 (1981): 88.

Sinha argues that these basic tenets are not found in Chinese, Japanese, African, Muslim, and Hindu societies. To provide one example, Sinha describes the process of Japanese law in the following way:

> However, in reality, the law made in imitation of the West governs a very small segment of social life which constitutes the presupposition of the Western law, namely, middle-class individuals fashioning their relations on the basis of freedom and liberty. *The majority of people still live according to the former ways and follow the Confucian idea based on natural order... since the notion of rights puts all persons on an equal basis, which is contrary to the Confucian hierarchy, it is deemed to depersonalize human relations. In the area of settlement of disputes, it is reconciliation which still enjoys a central place.*[37]

In any case, the inability of nature and reason, or human dignity and needs, to provide a universal foundation for human rights is clear. This leads to one of two possibilities. The first is to accept a plurality of human rights models, including those grounded in sacred texts and religious norms. The second option is to embrace the concept of relativity and to argue in favor of a single and universal human rights model based on changing sentiments and practical results. The next section looks at this second possibility in the form of the postmodern concept of ethical sentimentalism.

3.3. A critical exploration of ethical sentimentalism

Modern philosophers, such as Voltaire, Locke, and Kant, severed the connection between the traditional understanding of God from human nature and/or reason. They attempted to demonstrate that the latter two concepts were also transcendent and therefore universal. However, once human nature and reason were cut off from their ahistorical source in God, their presumed universality was heavily criticized. Following in the footsteps of Nietzsche (d.1900),[38] it did not take long for postmodern philosophers, such as Michel Foucault (d.1984) and Jacques Derrida (d.2004), to expose nature and reason as human constructs – relative and limited to their socio-

---

[37] Sinha, "Human Rights," 84. (Emphasis added)
[38] For Nietzsche's socio-historical and relative approach to morality, see Friedrich Nietzsche, *On the Genealogy of Morals and Ecce Homo*, trans. and ed. Walter A. Kaufmann (New York: Random House, 1989).

historical contexts.³⁹ Some human rights theorists, such as Jack Donnelley and Richard Rorty, argue that this postmodern shift in epistemology is not problematic in relation to human rights. For Donnelley, this is partly because there is no such thing as an essential human nature. Rather, according to him, human nature is a social project wherein humans construct their essential nature through social action. On this view, human rights is a prescriptive moral account; that is, it is a substantive model which provides a set of practices that allow people to develop their deeper moral nature.⁴⁰ In addition to this, Donnelley also argues that postmodern thought is not problematic for human rights theory because there is no such thing as an objective theoretical foundation for any belief. In this regard, he writes that

> Moral and political arguments require a firm place to stand. But that place appears firm largely because we have agreed to treat it as such. 'Foundations' 'ground' a theory only through an inescapably contentious decision to *define* such foundations as firm ground…There is no strong foundation for human rights – or, what amounts to the same thing, there are multiple, often inconsistent, 'foundations'…This is less of a problem than one might imagine.⁴¹

According to Donnelley, "this is less of a problem than one might imagine" for three reasons. First, this is because human rights are already 'relatively universal' to the extent that most nation-states have officially ratified international human rights law and consider it to be legally binding. However, it is exactly this lack of theoretical justification that makes it impossible to *fully actualize* human rights on a global scale. In other words, the problem with Donnelley's argument is that it ignores the immense political pressure placed on nation-states to accept human rights. The reality is that many nation-states formally endorse human rights because they cannot afford to do otherwise. This 'insincerity' is reflected in the countless human rights abuses carried out by countries that purportedly uphold international law. For example, Michael Freeman writes:

---

³⁹ Michael Foucault, *Power/Knowledge: Selected Interviews and other Writings 1972-1977*, trans. and ed. Colin Gordon (New York: Pantheon Books, 1997) and also see Jacques Derrida, *Writing and Difference*, trans. Alan Bass (Chicago: University of Chicago Press, 1980).
⁴⁰ Donnelly, *Universal Human Rights*, 7-23.
⁴¹ Donnelly, *Universal Human Rights*, 21.

The Vienna Conference of 1993 reinforced the commitment of the international community *in principle* to universal human rights. Most governments are *formally* committed to human rights. ...Yet serious violations continue...Human-rights scholars have begun to recognize that the global economy and the global climate may have massive implications for human rights.[42]

Thus, the 'relative universality' of human rights is strictly limited to its formal acceptance and not its practical application. Secondly, Donnelley argues that a lack of justification is "less of a problem than one might imagine" because human rights is a prescriptive model that should be judged by practical consequences and not theoretical soundness. Here, Donnelley is combining the deontological nature of human rights with the consequentialist nature of utilitarianism. The problem with this argument is that there is no tangible proof that human rights produce more positive consequences than negative ones. For example, global institutions, such as the World Bank, International Monetary Fund, and transnational corporations, use human rights to freely pursue and further their economic agendas. From this point of view, human rights are an empty bourgeoisie ideology that functions to pacify the working class and allows global powers to exploit poorer, 'southern' nation-states. Finally, Donnelley argues that a lack of 'grounding' is "less of a problem than one might imagine" because it makes human rights adaptable; it gives it the potential to be grounded in virtually every cultural tradition. However, this argument is based on the popular but false 'assumption of compartmentalization'. In other words, this argument assumes that human rights are 'minimalist' in nature; it assumes they can be implemented into different societies without disturbing those societies' respective worldviews and social realities. However, human rights is a theory of justice, and the latter is an integral part of every cultural tradition; therefore, changing a society's understanding of justice would mean changing that society's cultural institutions and behavioral norms. As the next section shows, the African, Chinese, and Islamic traditions have vastly different views concerning justice, and they cannot accept current international human rights without displacing their own ways of living. This is one of the reasons why these traditions are working towards formulating and adopting different human rights models – models that are more organic and integral to their own cultures and respective value systems.

---

[42] Freeman, *Human Rights*, 207. (Emphasis added)

Richard Rorty, to a large extent, adopts the same views as Donnelley. He also argues that there is no such thing as an essential human nature, and that human rights should be judged by their consequences and not their theoretical foundations. According to Rorty, postmodernists are made up of two general groups, that is, the cultural left and the progressive left. He criticizes the former for stopping the possibility of progress by not providing alternatives to the universal structures they deconstruct.[43] Rorty places himself among the progressive left, also known as the school of pragmatic postmodernism. In doing so, he puts forth a theory of human rights based on sentimentality.[44] In discussing Rorty's views, Michael Freeman writes:

> Rorty has argued that there is *no* theoretical foundation for human rights, because there is no theoretical *foundation* for any belief. This is not, however, something we should regret because it is a necessary philosophical truth, and because the cause of human rights does not require theory for its success, but, rather sympathy.[45]

Rorty's shift from theory to sympathy is in line with his general philosophical outlook. According to him, science and philosophy simply form a 'set of vocabularies' that change in relation to social convention and practicality; there is no reason to believe that our knowledge accurately represents a world that is independent of what we think. Defending the view that 'we cannot know anything' but 'we should still be moral' is a problem that postmodern philosophy faces in general; this is because the knowledge of 'anything' includes the knowledge of morality. In other words, morality loses its authority if it has no basis in a transcendent and knowable reality and is exclusively a product of changing social conventions. This essentially means that what is right in a particular socio-historical context can also be wrong in another. Of course, this view of morality clearly undermines human rights' claims to being universal, inalienable, and equal. In any case, Rorty's solution is to approach human rights with the postmodern theory of ethical sentimentalism. His argument is that ethics are a product of feelings in general and empathy in particular; therefore, they have nothing to do with knowledge or theory. In line with this, Rorty argues that human rights should be established through sentimental education – an

---

[43] Edward Grippe, "Richard Rorty," The Internet Encyclopedia of Philosophy: A Peer Reviewed, August 10, 2019, accessed https://www.iep.utm.edu/rorty/.

[44] Despite the views of Donnelley, Rorty, and the 'progressive left', postmodern theory largely criticizes human rights – and other universal ideologies – as false 'meta-narratives' that create abusive power structures which marginalize and oppress the 'Other'.

[45] Freeman, *Human Rights*, 62.

education that creates a feeling of empathy for other people's suffering.[46] Interestingly, Hunt's book – *Inventing Human Rights* – maps the historical processes by which social practices in the seventeenth and eighteenth centuries allowed people to empathize with the 'Other'. According to Hunt, these changes allowed for the human rights movement and the French and American revolutions. She writes:

> ...the newfound power of empathy could work against even the longest held prejudices...Neither autonomy nor empathy were fixed; they were skills that could be learned, and the 'acceptable' limitations on rights could be – and were – challenged. Rights cannot be defined once and for all because their emotional basis continues to shift...The human rights revolution is by definition ongoing.[47]

She continues:

> My argument will make much of the influence of new kinds of experiences, from viewing pictures in public exhibitions to reading the hugely popular epistolary novels about love and marriage. Such experiences helped spread the practices of autonomy and empathy...Each in their way reinforced the notion of a community based on autonomous, empathetic individuals who could be related beyond their immediate families, religious affiliations, or even action to greater universal values.[48]

The problem with ethical sentimentalism is its continually shifting point of reference. If human rights depend on what we feel, then it is only natural to ask what our feelings depend on. Although Hunt seems to 'celebrate' the shifting attitudes of the seventeenth and eighteenth centuries, it is obvious that these changes were –and continue to be – dangerously liable to manipulation by those who have control over public information.[49] For example, the media, whether in the form of an epistolary novel in the

---

[46] Richard Rorty, "Human Rights, Rationality, and Sentimentality," in *On Human Rights: The Oxford Amnesty Lectures*, ed. Stephen Shute and Susan Hurley (New York: Basic Books, 1993).
[47] Hunt, *Inventing Human Rights*, 28-29.
[48] Hunt, *Inventing Human Rights*, 32.
[49] For example, see Peter R. Mitchell and John Schoeffel, ed., *Understanding Power: The Indispensable Chomsky* (New York: The New Press, 2002).

seventeenth century or specific news outlets in the twenty-first century, can dictate who and what we feel empathy towards. According to George Soros,

> ...social media companies influence how people think and behave without them even being aware of it. This has far-reaching adverse consequences on the functioning of democracy... [In addition, social media companies] deceive their users by manipulating their attention and directing it towards their own commercial purposes [and] deliberately engineer addiction to the services they provide. The power to shape people's attention is increasingly concentrated in the hands of a few companies. It takes a real effort to assert and defend what John Stuart Mill called 'the freedom of mind'. There is a possibility that once lost, people who grow up in the digital age will have difficulty in regaining it. This may have far-reaching political consequences.[50]

Ethical sentimentalism aside, the greatest obstacle to the 'foundationless foundation' argument – much like utilitarianism and natural rights – is the problem of relativity. That is, the nonsensical notion that the only absolute is the relative. If there is no objective justification for anything, then the same argument applies to human rights. Moreover, if human rights are to be judged by their consequences, then what particular consequences will be judged and how will they be measured? Therefore, according to these postmodernists, there is no good reason to apply the concept of human rights; there is only the seemingly arbitrary decision to apply them. Moreover, the idea that there is no sound basis for any theoretical belief is based on an epistemological reductionism that limits human modes of knowing. More specifically, it is based on the particular concept of the human mind and reason that developed in the West between the fourteenth and eighteenth centuries. The second part of this study develops a theory of Islamic ethics and argues that it is possible to 'know reality'; therefore, it is possible to have an 'objective ground' for human rights.

This section critically surveyed some of the more popular ethical theories that claim to objectively justify the existence of human rights. It attempted to show that these theories do not adequately answer the 'question of foundations' and are unable to escape the problem of relativity. This is largely because international human rights are still a product of the secular-liberal

---

[50] Olivia Solon, "George Soros: Facebook and Google a Menace to Society," *The Guardian*, January 26, 2018, https://www.theguardian.com/business/2018/jan/25/george-soros-facebook-and-google-are-a-menace-to-society.

ethical tradition which reduces the transcendent to the worldly and denies the former altogether. Further testimony about the relative nature of human rights – in its current international formulation – is provided by critics from the African, Chinese, and Islamic traditions. The next section briefly looks at these critiques and the alternative visions they provide. The book then proceeds to the second part of the work which deals with human rights in relation to religion in general, and Islam in particular.

3.4. Human rights and the problem of universality

In this chapter, I have attempted to show that international human rights are far from universal. I have done this by pointing to the on-going and problematic debate from within the secular-liberal tradition concerning the ethical foundation of human rights. This wide spread disagreement is sufficient evidence for the relative nature of contemporary human rights norms. This evidence is further strengthened when it is combined with criticism being produced from outside of the secular-liberal tradition. In particular, it is strengthened by critiques coming from activists and theorists working within the African, Asian, and Islamic traditions. Many of these places are part of the 'global south', and their arguments are based on both economics and culture. Rhonda Callaway and Julie Harrelson-Stephens succinctly summarize their position by writing that

> Developing countries are quick to dispute the universality of human rights, arguing three main points. First, developing countries had little input in the drafting of the document due to their colonial position at the time. Second, these same countries contend that the rights outlined in the declaration are ethnocentric, reflecting Western conceptions and omitting non-Western views on human rights. Last, critics contend that too much emphasis is placed on the rights of the individual often at the expense of the rights of groups and collectivities.[51]

In the case of Asia for example, some critics argue that the liberal emphasis on the primacy of the individual and autonomy opposes the Asian emphasis on

---

[51] Rhonda Callaway and Julie Harrelson-Stephens, "What are human rights? Definitions and typologies of Today's Human Rights Discourse," in *Exploring International Human Rights: Essential Readings*, ed. Rhonda L. Callaway and Julie Harrelson-Stephens (London: Lynne Rienner Publishers, 2007), 8.

the primacy of the family and stability.[52,53] In light of this, they argue in favor of a strong centralized government that establishes order and harmony. According to proponents of 'Asian values', order is necessary for economic success and the actual freedom and enjoyment of rights. In this regard, Lee Kuan Yew (d.2015), the former prime minister of Singapore, stated:

> We used the family to push economic growth, factoring the ambitions of a person and his family into our planning…The government can create a setting in which people can live happily and succeed and express themselves, but finally it is what people do with their lives that determines economic success or failure. Again, we are fortunate we had this cultural backdrop, the belief in thrift, hard work, filial piety, and loyalty in the extended family, and, most of all, respect for scholarship and learning.[54]

Some of the values that he mentions are based on Confucianism – a worldview that has dominated much of the far-East and highly influenced its people and their way of life.[55] Yew, like many other proponents of 'Asian values', also connects the issue of international human rights with the perceived moral decay of the West:

> As a total system, I find parts of it totally unacceptable: guns, drugs, violent crimes, vagrancy, unbecoming behavior in public – in sum, the breakdown of civil society. The expansion of the right of the individual to behave or misbehave as he pleases has come at the expense of orderly society. In the East the main object is to have a well-ordered society so that everybody can have maximum enjoyment of his freedoms.[56]

---

[52] For example, articles 17 and 21 in the "Universal Declaration". These two articles suggest the Western economic and political institutions of capitalism and democracy respectively.

[53] No cultural tradition is a monolith; therefore, this is not the view of all 'Asian peoples'. Of course, the same can be said of both Western and non-Western traditions.

[54] As quoted in Rhonda L. Callaway, "The Rhetoric of Asian Values," in *Exploring International Human Rights: Essential Readings*, ed. Rhonda L. Callaway and Julie Harrelson-Stephens (London: Lynne Rienner Publishers, 2007), 116.

[55] See Theodore De Barry and Tu Weiming, ed., *Confucianism and Human Rights* (New York: Columbia University Press, 1997).

[56] As quoted in Callaway, "Rhetoric," 113.

Therefore, critics of universalism argue that the wholesale implementation of rights, as expressed in the International Bill of Rights, would effectively debase the Asian tradition and its rich cultural history. The same or similar arguments are given by some groups from the African and Islamic traditions. In the case of Africa for example, Shashi Tharoor writes about the cultural importance of community and the primacy of the values of respect, restraint, responsibility and reciprocity:

> ...in Africa it is the community that protects and nurtures the individual. One African writer summed up the African philosophy of existence as: "I am because we are, and because we are therefore I am." Some Africans have argued that they have a complex structure of communal entitlements and obligations grouped around what one might call four "r's": not "rights," but respect, restraint, responsibility, and reciprocity. They argue that in most African societies group rights have always taken precedence over individual rights, and political decisions have been made through group consensus, not through individual assertions of rights.[57]

Thus, the preamble to the African Charter on Human and Peoples' Rights states:

> *Taking into consideration* the virtues of their historical tradition and the values of African civilization which should inspire and characterize their reflection on the concept of human and peoples' rights... [and] *considering* that the enjoyment of rights and freedoms also implies the performance of duties on the part of everyone.[58]

Finally, the same arguments based on cultural differences is made by Middle-Eastern theorists in general, and those influenced by the Islamic tradition in particular. The following chapters provide a more in-depth analysis of the issue of Islam and human rights. For the moment, it suffices to point out Muslim societies – despite the pervasiveness of liberal ideologies – still hold a worldview and value-system grounded in the Quran, hadith, and Islamic

---

[57] Sashi Tharoor, "Are Human Rights Universal?," *World Policy Journal* 16, no. 4 (1999-2000): 1-6.
[58] See the preamble in the "African Charter on Human and Peoples' Rights," African Commission on Human and Peoples' Rights, accessed July 10, 2019, https://www.achpr.org/legalinstruments/detail?id=49#:~:text=The%20African%20Charter%20on%20Human,freedoms%20in%20the%20African%20continent.

intellectual history. Nasr, a prominent proponent of the school of Islamic traditionalism, states:

> In today's world everyone speaks of human rights and the sacred character of human life, and many secularists even claim that they are the true champions of human rights...But strangely enough, often those same champions of humanity believe that human beings are nothing more than evolved apes...If the human being is nothing but the result of 'blind forces'...then is not the very statement of the sacredness of human life intellectually meaningless and nothing but a hollow sentiment of expression?[59]

Thus, the preamble to The Universal Islamic Declaration of Human Rights states:

> Whereas Allah (God) has given mankind through His revelation in the Holy Quran and the Sunnah of His blessed Prophet Muhammad an abiding legal and moral framework within which to establish and regulate human relationships.

and

> Whereas by virtue of their Divine source and sanction these rights can neither be curtailed, abrogated or disregarded by authorities, assemblies or other institutions, nor can they be surrendered or alienated.[60]

To reiterate, according to Sinha, all three of these traditions have a worldview with at least three things in common. First, they agree that the fundamental unit of society is the family rather than the individual. Second, they believe that the primary basis for securing human existence is through duties rather than rights. Lastly, they maintain that the primary method of securing rights is through reconciliation, repentance, or education as opposed to procedural legalism.[61] These three cultural traditions' claim that the Universal Declaration is eurocentric is augmented by the fact that they have produced their own human rights treatises. The Asian-Pacific regions drafted and

---

[59] Seyyed Hossein Nasr, *The Heart of Islam: Enduring Values for Humanity* (New York: HarperCollins, 2002), 275.
[60] See the Preamble in the "Universal Islamic Declaration of Human Rights," Al-Hewar Center, accessed July 11, 2019, http://www.alhewar.com/ISLAMDECL.html.
[61] Sinha, "Human Rights," 77.

adopted the Asean Declaration in 1993; the Organization of African Unity – now the African Union – drafted and adopted the African Charter on Human and Peoples' Rights in 1981; and the Islamic Council drafted the Universal Islamic Declaration of Human Rights in 1981. In addition to this, in 1997, the InterAction Council responded to the current emphasis on rights by drafting the Universal Declaration of Human Responsibilities. However, the fact that contemporary international human rights are clearly not universal, does not negate the concept of universality altogether. Although many of these critiques point to the uniqueness of their own cultural traditions, they also mention points of convergence. For example, in addressing the contemporary African approach to human rights, Ibhawoh writes that

> The Africanist approach to the discourse on the cultural relativism of human rights can...be broadly dived into two schools. The first of these is the less radical approach...Proponents of this school, while arguing the validity of a uniquely African concept of human rights, also recognize the universality of a basic core of human rights. Kofi Quashigah (1991) for instance, concludes that human rights concepts, which are rooted in certain social facts that are peculiar to particular societies, cannot be expected to be universal. At the same time, he acknowledges that certain basic needs are indisputably ascribable to persons of every...background.[62]

As mentioned, this work belongs to pluralist-universal school of human rights and attempts to negotiate a middle position between modernism's universalism and postmodernism's relativism. Modernism refers to the ideology that grew out of the Renaissance and Reformation movements in the West. It is generally characterized by a belief in progress, science, and reason. Moreover, modernism focuses on individual autonomy, and it believes in the possibility of universal ethics and a unified global society. Therefore, most advocates of universal human rights belong to the modern tradition.[63] On the other end of the spectrum is postmodernism, which is largely a reaction to – and deconstruction of – modernism. It is largely characterized by its emphasis on relativism and its stance against 'meta-narratives', that is, theories that claim to give

---

[62] Ibhawoh, "Restraining Universalism," 133-134. Also see Abdullah An-Na'mi, ed., *Human Rights in Cross-Cultural Perspectives: A Quest for Consensus* (Philadelphia: University of Pennsylvania Press, 1992).
[63] Habermas is arguably the most influential theorist's belonging to the modern tradition today. For an introduction to his work, see James G. Finlayson, *Habermas: A Very Short Introduction* (Oxford: Oxford University Press, 2005).

comprehensive accounts based on universal truths. Postmodernism's deconstruction of 'absolute truths' is in line with one of its central aims, that is, the deconstruction of power structures that allow for the marginalization and oppression of minorities.[64] This in turn, is also closely related to 'Saidian Orientalism' – a post-colonial philosophy that also rejects modernism's approach to the 'Other'. Its criticism is mainly aimed at the Western orientalists who have a tendency to essentialize other cultures as monolithic, static, and primitive. For post-colonial theorists, this false construct is problematic because it implicitly or explicitly argues for the superiority of the West and the need to 'correct' other cultures through colonization and/or intervention. Edward Said's "Islam through Western Eyes" states:

> How fundamentally narrow and constricted is the semantic field of Islam was brought home to me after my book *Orientalism* appeared last year. Even though I took great pains in the book to show that current discussions of the Orient or of the Arabs and Islam are fundamentally premised upon a fiction, my book was often interpreted as a defense of the "real" Islam. Whereas what I was trying to show was that any talk about Islam was radically flawed, not only because an unwarranted assumption was being made that a large ideologically freighted generalization could cover all the rich and diverse particularity of Islamic *life* (a very different thing) but also because it would simply be repeating the errors of Orientalism to claim that the correct view of Islam was X or Y or Z.[65]

Thus, advocates of culturally relative rights generally belong to the postmodern and post-colonial traditions.[66] In challenging the relativity and universality of human rights, this book adopts the Rawlsian notion of a 'minimal overlapping consensus'.[67] For example, "Rawls…held that only Articles 3-18 represent genuine human rights because the other rights are

---

[64] For example, see Michael Foucault, *Discipline and Punish: The Birth of the Prison*, 2nd ed., trans. Alan Sheridan (New York: Vintage Books, 1995).
[65] Edward W. Said, "Islam Through Western Eyes," *The Nation*, April 26, 1980, https://www.thenation.com/article/archive/islam-through-western-eyes/.
[66] That is if they believe in human rights at all. Most postmodernists and post-colonialists argue that the concept itself is a false human construct that allows for unfair social relations and power structures.
[67] This study argues that a 'minimal overlapping consensus' is both possible and desirable. However, it does not agree with Rawls' theoretical approach in general, nor its assumptions in particular.

either liberal, and therefore not universizable, or presuppose particular institutions."[68] Therefore, as Kao points out, "Rawls' toleration of a type of non-liberal society that he calls 'decent' leads him to reject an articulation of human rights that would be 'peculiarly liberal or special to the Western Tradition'."[69] However, it is important to reiterate that, in my opinion, any overlapping consensus between cultural traditions should be accidental and not essential in nature. This would ensure that rights are not forced onto a particular culture and its specific way of life. At the same time, however, any 'overlapping rights' would become 'essential' in the sense that their general acceptance would make up the core of what could rightly be called 'universal' human rights.

In conclusion, the first part of this book argues that international human rights are not truly universal because they are underpinned by the modern-liberal principles of universalism, individualism, secularism, and the like. This conclusion is based on a critical examination of popular human rights histories; contemporary ethical theories; and human rights' views from other cultural traditions. This general argument is made more specific in the following chapters, which considers the possibility of grounding human rights within a religious framework. Thus, this book breaks off from its current discussion and moves on to examine the relationship between human rights and religion in general, and the issue of human rights and Islam in particular.

---

[68] Freeman, *Human Rights*, 75.
[69] Kao, *Grounding Human Rights*, 58.

Chapter 4

Religion, Islam, and Human Rights

What is the relationship between religion and human rights? One answer to this question – and arguably the most common – is that religion and human rights are diametrically opposed to one another.[1] This view runs parallel to the popular histories describing the rise of international rights: religious societies – particularly before the fourteenth century – were duty-based, hierarchical, and undemocratic; they maintained a worldview and subsequent social order that was elitist and oppressive towards the general public.[2] For example, Lauren writes that "...The overwhelming majority of all human beings who ever lived...did so under some form of...human rights violations... Human bondage was common...[and] prejudice and discrimination prevailed." This view of premodern societies is then juxtaposed with human rights societies. The latter, despite their admitted shortcomings, are described as humane, progressive, and liberal. Thus, proponents of this view understand the narrative of human rights as "one of traditional religious authority opposed to the secular Enlightenment ideal of rational, autonomous individuals as bearers of universal rights."[3] They justify their position by pointing to a number of 'progressive' modern developments, such as those in the fields of health science, technology, and economics. Mostly, however, they point to the rise of the concept of human rights itself; the increasingly fashionable idea that all human beings are inherently equal and entitled to the same subjective rights. Donnelley, for example, argues that liberal societies and their concomitant human rights norms have superseded religion as the favored structure of society and theory of justice respectively. According to him, there are three stages that a society goes through before becoming a human rights society proper: liberalization, democratization, and finally, a rights-protective regime. For Donnelley, this final society is a liberal democracy.[4] In this regard, many human rights proponents adopt the Frazarian view of progress and

---

[1] This position is promulgated by figures such as Jack Donnelly, Louis Jenkins and Jacob Burckhardt. On this 'dominant narrative', see Banchoff and Wuthnow, "Introduction," 2-4.
[2] Lauren, "History of Human Rights," 394.
[3] Banchoff and Wuthnow, "Introduction," 4.
[4] Jack Donnelly, "The Relative Universality of Human Rights," *Human Rights Quarterly* 29, no. 2 (2007): 281-306.

maintain that religions acted as a 'stepping stone' towards the fulfilment of a new international human rights regime; a secular regime based on reason and not a religious regime based on revelation.[5] In any case, according to this view, the right to 'freedom of religion' is reduced to exclude religious actors and forces from being a source of public policy. Freedom is only applied to private, non-intrusive, and individual faith. If a particular faith-group does invoke revelation, they are forced to rationalize their invocation and, in doing so, reduce the latter to the rational faculty. In other words, they are forced to assume an epistemological model wherein rationality sits at the apex and revelation falls somewhere below it. This political setup follows in the footsteps of Rawls who argued that, in liberal democracies, 'reasonable people' would allow everyone to follow their faith, but they would only rely on what was reasonable in the public sphere.[6,7] Louis Henkin aptly summarizes this answer by categorizing the differences between religion and human rights into four parts. He writes that the two ideologies differ when it comes to their sources, authority, expressive forms, and substantive norms. For example, in terms of their sources and authority, Henkin writes:

> Religion and religions…see their moral code as part of a total cosmic order and as emanating from a Supreme Legislator. The Supreme Legislator, directly or through authorized representatives, has prescribed a moral code of human behaviour in an authoritative text…By contrast, in its contemporary articulation, the human rights ideology, aiming at universality (and developed during years when half the political world was committed to atheism), has eschewed invoking any theistic authority… It has avoided rooting itself in any story of human origins, or even in "natural" law or "natural" rights. The human rights ideology does not see human rights as integral to a cosmic order. It does not derive from any sacred text. Its sources are human, deriving from contemporary human life in human society.[8]

---

[5] It is important to note that Donnelly in particular does not trace back human 'progress' to religion; rather, he traces it back to the construction of liberal democracies and the Universal Declaration.
[6] Kao, *Grounding Human Rights*, 57-76.
[7] Here, I am referring to Rawls' ideal public sphere which is characterized by three principal features: liberalism, secularism, and rationalism.
[8] Louis Henkin, "Religion, Religions and Human Rights," *The Journal of Religious Ethics* 26, no. 2 (1998): 229-39.

Another answer concerning the relationship between religion and human rights is that the two are only somewhat compatible with one another. This answer tends to come from those who understand contemporary human rights as a product of the Renaissance, Reformation, and Enlightenment periods in the West. They understand that these periods of history largely rejected traditional religion, doctrine, and rituals in favor of modern and humanistic ideologies. For example, Harry Oldmeadow writes:

> The Renaissance, the Scientific Revolution, and the Enlightenment were all incubators of ideas and values which first decimated Christendom and then spread throughout the world… Behind the proliferating ideologies of the last few centuries we can discern an ignorance of ultimate realities and an indifference…to the eternal verities conveyed by Tradition.[9]

Advocates of this view maintain that many of the ideologies that underpin the Universal Declaration are decidedly anti-religious and anti-traditional. These ideologies include, for example, secularism and its replacement of faith in God with faith in the autonomous-rational human being. However, they do not reject human rights altogether. This is because religion has always been concerned with the concept of justice in general, and ethical conduct among human beings in particular.[10] Rather, they argue that human rights-based on religious principles would be somewhat different than those rights that are considered to be 'universal' today. For example, after explaining that responsibilities precede rights in the Islamic tradition, Nasr goes on to write the following:

> Turning to the more specific question of human rights as currently understood in the West, according to Islam… The first rights of human beings concern their immortal souls. Men and women have the right to seek the salvation of their souls, which Islam, like other religions, considers our first duty toward ourselves and toward God…[11]

---

[9] Harry Oldmeadow, *Frithjof Schuon and the Perennial Philosophy* (Bloomington: World Wisdom, 2010), 215.
[10] Despite the differences between premodern and modern understandings of justice and ethics, agreement can be found through dialogue and the inclusion of different human rights models.
[11] Nasr, *Heart of Islam*, 282.

The first answer, which maintains that religion and human rights are incompatible, tends to portray the two as fixed ideologies, and it ignores their significant overlap in theory and practice. In part, this is because it assumes that religion cannot add anything to forward the cause of human rights and/or vice versa. The second answer argues that both points of view are dynamic with boundaries that are constantly being negotiated and/or reframed. In the same light, this study argues for a 'middle ground' and insists that the two can find some 'spaces of convergence' on the condition that they are willing to engage with each other. A dialogical approach is important because "it aids with understanding persons from different traditions and cultures than one's own because it recognizes those persons as agents"[12] and that "...to understand others as agents requires that we view them as possessing self-understanding rather than unilaterally categorize them as mere objects of study."[13] Some human rights theorists, such as Ignatieff, argue that any kind of dialogue and compromise is unnecessary because the Universal Declaration sufficiently represents the world's religions and cultural traditions. This is because the commission's primary goal was to create a declaration that was globally inclusive in scope. Moreover, the drafters were chosen with this goal in mind and they clearly believed they succeeded. The declaration reads:

> Now therefore, the GENERAL ASSEMBLY proclaims this UNIVERSAL DECLARATION OF HUMAN RIGHTS as a common standard of achievement for all peoples and all nations, to the end that every individual and every organ of society, keeping this declaration constantly in mind, shall strive by teaching and education to promote respect for these rights and freedoms and by progressive measures, nation and international, to secure their universal and effective recognition and observance, both among the peoples of the Member States themselves and among the peoples of territories under their jurisdiction.[14]

However, this representation was highly suspect, and traditional voices were, and also continue to be, conspicuously absent. For example, Charles Malik – the Christian-Lebanese representative – received his education from a number of Western universities. He was a philosopher and diplomat, and he served as the Lebanese minister of Education and Fine Arts and the Minister of Foreign Affairs. Similarly, Peng-Chun Chan – the Chinese-Confucian

---

[12] Oh, *Rights of God*, 2.
[13] Oh, *Rights of God*, 2.
[14] "Universal Declaration."

representative – graduated from Columbia University, and he taught at the University of Chicago. He was a playwright, philosopher, and diplomat. This type of background applies to many of the drafters who represented a liberal minority within their respective traditions.[15] Of course, the issue does not concern the specific education and/or vocation of the drafters. Rather, as Sachedina points out,

> It is quite revealing that Muslim participation was minimalist in the sense that there was no real effort to expound comprehensive Islamic doctrines to get the sense of the tradition's stance on different articles. Further, as the profile of the different representatives from participating Muslim countries like Saudi Arabia, Pakistan and Syria reveals, *the representatives from Muslim countries were peculiarly educated individuals, who had little or no human rights training in the foundational sources of Islamic tradition...*[16]

In addition to this, Ignatieff and Morsink, who are both proponents of the Declaration's universality, are forced to admit that its creation was, at least to some extent, a one-sided affair. For example, Morsink writes that "this process [of drafting the declaration] was dominated by nations from around the North Atlantic...and from Latin America, and that large regions of our world, such as Asia and Africa, were grossly underrepresented at the drafting table."[17] Ignatieff also admits that the process was directed by Western thinkers and norms; however, he argues that this didn't lead to any form of moral imperialism because their attitude was "anything but triumphant" in light of the World War.[18] Finally, it is also important to remember that the drafters did not agree on many foundational issues; thus, their consensus was strictly limited to the practical sphere.

In any case, the view that religion and human rights are completely at odds is losing its dominance. On both sides, there are people attempting to reframe, reinterpret, and/or expand their respective doctrines in search of a synthesis of sorts. This movement's importance cannot be brushed aside. As Oh writes in the case of Islam:

---

[15] For a background of the drafters, see Morsink, *The Universal Declaration*, 1-28.
[16] Sachedina, *Islam and the Challenge*, 10-11. (Emphasis added.)
[17] Morsink, *The Universal Declaration*, 36.
[18] Ignatieff, "Attack on Human Rights."

Although the foundations of human rights may be debated, human rights scholars cannot easily dismiss the potential that foundational beliefs, including Islam, hold in advancing human rights agendas. After all, approximately one billion inhabitants of this earth identify themselves as Muslim. To ignore the values of Islam would be to deny the voices of one-fifth of the world's population in determining what should be "universal" human rights.[19]

I agree with the second response, that is, that religion(s) and human rights partially overlap in theory and in practice. Moreover, I argue that international human cannot afford to ignore religion for two reasons. The first is that for religious people, the foundational belief in the Absolute is the only thing that can ground and validate human rights. The second reason is the so-called 'religious resurgence' and its testimony that a large part of the world's population still wants to live according to their sacred texts and traditional norms.[20] This means that international human rights need to be more flexible and inclusive of different human rights visions. It also means that religious societies should be free to develop their own models that share the goal of curbing excess of power and entitling citizens to pursue their particular society's conception of 'the good'. In this regard, I agree with the Asean declaration, to the extent that it stresses

> The urgent need to democratize the United Nations system, eliminate selectivity and improve procedures and mechanisms in order to strengthen international cooperation, based on principles of equality and mutual respect, and ensure a positive, balanced and non-confrontational approach in addressing and realizing all aspects of human rights.[21]

To this end, my work is specifically concerned with the Islamic intellectual tradition and its worldview, as expressed by the school of Islamic traditionalism. I begin by looking at 'Islam and the challenge of human rights', and by critically exploring some of the contemporary Muslim responses to the issues at hand. Finally, I go on to develop a theory of virtue ethics with the potential to 'ground' an Islamic model of human rights.

---

[19] Oh, *Rights of God*, 1.
[20] Sinha, "Human Rights."
[21] "Asean Human Rights Declaration," Association of Southeast Asian Nations, July 21, 2019, accessed https://asean.org/asean-human-rights-declaration/.

4.1. Islam and the challenge of human rights

The eighteenth century witnessed the beginning of the end of the Islamic empire. The Muslim world was colonized, and their systems of government were replaced by secular institutions modeled after the West.[22] These models, which remained in place after the 'independence' of Muslim lands, failed to bring the economic prosperity and social stability they promised.[23] This was due to internal corruption and hypocritical foreign policy, and it resulted in a growing resentment of the Western world and a search for new answers. One of these answers was the return to an Islamic society that was legitimized by the implementation of the shariah. Shariah literally means 'path to water', and it is commonly translated as Islamic law. However, the shariah doesn't exclusively deal with the law; it is much broader and provides guidance and governance for all aspects of Muslim life.[24] In this way, for many Muslims, it transforms the mundane into the sacred and serves as a reminder of God's near and everlasting presence.[25] Noah Feldman aptly explains the phenomenon of 'Islamism' by connecting it to the shariah:

> In essence, then, the call for an Islamic state is the call for the establishment of Islamic law. Once we take this demand seriously, we can begin to understand why so many people in the Muslim world find themselves attracted to Islamic politics. Looking at their own states, they see that power, not law, is structuring political, economic and social relations. Law sounds as though it might be the solution. What is more, law seems to hold particularly great promise because, in the collective memory of the Muslim world, it is still dimly remembered that the classical state was a state that was governed by law and that governed through law.[26]

---

[22] Some Islamic societies were never directly colonized. Nevertheless, they have not escaped phenomenon of globalization, and they currently face many of the same problems as other Muslim-majority nation-states.
[23] In general, see Loomba, *Colonialism/Postcolonialism*.
[24] For a general overview see Devin J. Stewart, "Shari'a," in *The Princeton Encyclopedia of Islamic Political Thought*, ed. Gerhard Bowering, Patricia Crone, Wadad Kadi, Devin J. Stewart, Muhammed Qasim Zaman and Mahan Mirza (Princeton: Princeton University Press, 2013), 497-505.
[25] S. H. Nasr, *Ideals and Realities of Islam* (Illinois: ABC International Group, 2000), 85-113.
[26] Noah Feldman, *The Fall and Rise of the Islamic State* (Princeton: Princeton University Press, 2008), 21.

Here, a brief summary of the development of Islamic law is necessary in order to provide the context for the following section on contemporary Islamic thought in general, and the progressive Muslim school's approach to Islamic law and human rights in particular.

During the lifetime of the Prophet, the Islamic community did not need to develop a legal science; the Prophet's authority as the Messenger of God extended over all areas. He was considered *the* religious, political, and moral guide. In this regard, the Qur'an reads:

> These are Allah's bounds, and whoever obeys Allah and His Apostle, He shall admit him to gardens with streams running in them, to remain in them [forever]. (4:13)

> All the response of the faithful, when they are summoned to Allah and His Apostle that He may judge between them, is to say, 'We hear and obey.' It is they who are the felicitous. (24:51)

> Whoever obeys Allah and the Apostle—they are with those whom Allah has blessed, including the prophets and the truthful, the martyrs and the righteous, and excellent companions are they! (4:69)

Thus, the newly emerging Islamic community generally referred to the Prophet when they faced any contentious issues. However, the death of the Prophet and subsequent spread of the Islamic empire necessitated the development of an Islamic legal system; the Muslim community was looking for answers to questions that were not directly addressed by the Quran or the Prophet. Initially, there was much debate concerning the principles and the sources of law (*uṣūl al-fiqh*), as well as the latter's relationship to one another. For example, the concept of religious custom or practice (*sunna*) originally extended beyond the Prophet's words and actions as recorded in the hadith literature. It included the personal opinions (*ra'y*) and customs (*'ādāt*) of the Caliphs and the Prophet's companions on the basis that the latter two had intimate knowledge of the Prophet; therefore, they could rightly ascertain what he would have done in any given situation.[27] Some legal scholars extended the same idea to the city of Medina; they believed that the city's way of life was modeled after the Prophet, therefore, it could act as a general guide

---

[27] Wael Hallaq, *The Origins and Evolution of Islamic Law* (New York: Cambridge University Press, 2005), 54-56.

and source of law for correct action.[28] Eventually, by the ninth and tenth Islamic centuries, Islamic law developed into a distinct field; the jurists, for the most part, agreed on the sources of law and consolidated them into a working system. Imam Muḥammad al-Shāfiʿī (d.820) is normally considered to be the most significant figure in this movement. He argued that the primary sources of law were the Quran and Prophetic Sunna contained within the hadith corpus.[29] He distinguished and elevated the latter's status by highlighting passages of the Quran that placed the Prophet above other people as a source of guidance. For example:

> Take whatever the Apostle gives you, and refrain from whatever he forbids you, and be wary of Allah. Indeed Allah is severe in retribution. (59:07)

> There is certainly a good exemplar for you in the Apostle of Allah—for those who look forward to Allah and the Last Day, and remember Allah much. (33:21)

> O you who have faith! Obey Allah and obey the Apostle and those vested with authority among you. And if you dispute concerning anything, refer it to Allah and the Apostle, if you have faith in Allah and the Last Day. That is better and more favourable in outcome. (4:59)

Al-Shāfiʿī's main legal concern was centralizing the hadith of the Prophet as the main source of Sunna, and limiting, as much as possible, human intervention in mediating Divine injunctions. If the primary sources of the Quran and Sunna did not provide an answer to a question, then one could turn to the secondary sources. The first of these was the consensus of the scholars (*ijmāʿ*), and the second and final source was analogical reasoning (*qiyās*) based on the Quran and the hadith. In regard to the typology of sources, Hallaq writes:

> …There was no question in the legal theory that emerged during the fourth/tenth century as to the correct hierarchy of legal sources. The Qur'an came first, at least formally and in terms of prestige and sanctity. The Sunna, wholly represented by *ḥadīth*, formed the second material source of the law, followed, in order of importance, by consensus and

---

[28] Hallaq, *Origins and Evolution*, 45-46.
[29] Hallaq, *Origins and Evolution*, 117-19.

qiyās. The first two may be described as material sources, while the latter two…are procedural, drawing from the former.[30]

Thus, by the tenth century, four schools of law crystallized in the Sunni world. Their eponyms were Imams Abū Ḥanīfa (d.767), Mālik b. Anas (d.796), Muḥammad al-Shāfiʿī (d.820), and Aḥmad b. Ḥanbal (d.855). In addition to this, there was the codification of the Shia school of law that was largely based on the teachings of their sixth Imam, Jaʿfar al-Ṣādiq (d.765).[31] The five schools did not place similar emphasis on the legal sources. For example, the Hanbali school was more conservative and generally stayed away from independent and analogical reasoning. In any case, the legal scholars played an extremely significant role in Muslim societies. They provided legitimacy to the ruling power of their time and also functioned as a check and balance to that same power. In this sense, they worked as a living constitution of sorts. Feldman's *The Fall and Rise of the Islamic State* probes into the nature of this development. He asks,

> How did this arrangement come about? How did the scholars, men with little direct political power, no armies, and often no government posts, become the sole keepers of the shari'a, and hence the only meaningful check on the power of the ruler? The answer goes back to the way Islamic law itself developed alongside the Islamic state.[32]

Feldman goes on to rightly explain that the Prophet had religious and political power over the community and when he died that power was assumed by the caliphs. Eventually, however, the caliphs were unable to provide the religious guidance that the community needed.[33] This, in turn, opened the door for the religious scholars – men who were well trained in the study of hadith and could tell the people what the Prophet would have done in similar circumstances.[34] This system, with its self-balancing structures of power,

---

[30] Hallaq, *Origins and Evolution*, 119.
[31] Mohammad H. Kamali, *Shari'ah Law: An Introduction* (Oxford: Oneworld Publications, 2008), 246-49.
[32] Feldman, *Fall and Rise*, 23.
[33] This refers to the caliphs of the Umayyad and Abbasid dynasties and not to the first four Caliphs.
[34] Feldman, *The Fall and Rise*, 23-5.

successfully kept the Islamic world functioning for centuries.³⁵ It is not a surprise then, that today's Muslims should look to the past when facing problems within their own Muslim-majority nation-states. However, many people, particularly those from within the secular-liberal tradition, remain suspicious of a legal system based on religion and its socio-legal norms. Echoing popular sentiments, Elizabeth Ann Mayer clearly outlines her assumptions and states:

> I believe in the normative character of the human rights principles set forth in international law and their universality... This inclines me to be critical of any actual or proposed governmental rights policies that violate international human rights law, regardless of whether they employ secular rationales or Islamic doctrines as justifications... as a supporter of international human law and an advocate for respect for human rights, I readily concede that I regard liberal reformist trends in Islamic thought as positive developments.³⁶

More specifically, there are at least three areas within the field of traditional Islamic jurisprudence that are considered to be antithetical to the concept of contemporary human rights. These are its stance on gender, non-Muslims, and its penal code. Before proceeding, however, it is important to note that this work is not a study in traditional Islamic law in all of its nuance and complexity. It is primarily concerned with ethics in light of the school of Islamic traditionalism and the latter's concept of virtue. Therefore, this chapter's objective is to simply 'points towards' the general areas of friction between traditional Islamic law and contemporary human rights.

In the case of gender, the main issue concerns the relationship between men and women and their differential treatment before the law. According to many Muslims, men and women have different natures; therefore, they have different God-given roles and duties. According to this view, justice requires understanding these natural differences and deriving and applying laws

---

³⁵ According to Majid Khadduri, this system was a Divine Nomocracy. He writes, "It is therefore the Law, embodying the principles of Divine Authority, which indeed rules and therefore the state becomes not, strictly speaking, a theocracy, but a form of nomocracy. The Islamic State, whose constitution and source of authority is Divine Law, might be called a Divine nomocracy." Khadduri, *Islamic Conception*, 4.

³⁶ Ann E. Mayer, *Islam and Human Rights: Tradition and Politics*, 3rd ed. (Colorado: Westview Press.1999), xvi.

accordingly. This traditional understanding of gender is based on the Quran, hadith, and Islamic intellectual tradition.[37] For example, the Quran reads:

> Divorced women shall wait by themselves for three periods of purity [after menses], and it is not lawful for them to conceal what Allah has created in their wombs if they believe in Allah and the Last Day; and their husbands have a greater right to restore them during this [duration], if they desire reconcilement. The wives have rights similar to the obligations upon them, in accordance with honourable norms; and men have a degree above them, and Allah is all-mighty and all-wise. (2:228)

> Men are the managers of women, because of the advantage Allah has granted some of them over others, and by virtue of their spending out of their wealth. Righteous women are obedient and watchful in the absence [of their husbands] in guarding what Allah has enjoined [them] to guard. As for those [wives] whose misconduct you fear, [first] advise them, and [if ineffective] keep away from them in the bed, and [as the last resort] beat them. Then if they obey you, do not seek any course [of action] against them. Indeed Allah is all-exalted, all-great. (04:34)

Many traditional commentaries maintain that these types of verses point to contextual *and* ontological differences between the two genders. For example, in relation to verse 4:34, *The Study Quran* refers to the commentaries of ibn Kathīr, Ḥusayn Ṭabāṭabāʿī and al-Qurṭubi and states:

> Many commentaries also claimed…that the ["more"] that God has given to men includes spiritual and worldly distinctions not necessarily related to financial matters. Among the distinctions they consider to have been given, if not exclusively, at least in many cases in greater measure to men are…authority, strength and the responsibility of *jihad*; some also assert that all prophets and most scholars…were men.[38]

Of course, as the following section on contemporary Islamic thought demonstrates, it can be argued that these verses are conditional and no longer apply today. However, to reiterate, this section is strictly concerned with

---

[37] In terms of Islamic traditionalism and the feminine, see Patrick Laude, *Pathways to an Inner Islam: Massignon, Corbin, Guenon and Schuon* (Albany: State University of New York Press, 2010), 103-26.

[38] Nasr et al., *The Study Quran*, 206-7.

drawing out the general friction between human rights and traditional Islamic law. Hence, the point remains: Islamic law reflects the Islamic intellectual tradition's understanding of gender differences, and this law is in friction with current international human rights norms.[39]

The second space of friction between human rights and Islamic law concern's the latter's marginalization and oppression of non-Muslims. Islamic history is full of instances where Muslims peacefully coexisted with peoples of other faiths. Conversely, it is also full of instances where Muslims oppressed and subjugated non-Muslims. The Quran, due to the fact that it was revealed in different contexts, can be used to justify both positions. In terms of differential treatment, for example, verse 9:29 reads:

> Fight those who do not have faith in Allah or believe in the Last Day, nor forbid what Allah and His Messenger have forbidden, nor practise the true religion, from among those who were given the Book, until they pay the tribute and feel themselves subdued. (9:29)[40]

Jizyah was an indemnity or financial tribute that non-Muslims paid to the Islamic state based on a mutual contract. Thus, the religious groups that paid the *jizyah* were also referred to as the 'people of the contract' (*ahl al-dhimmi*).[41] These groups, which included the Christians and Jews, were sometimes treated as second-class members of the state. According to Caner Dagali's commentary of verse 9:29,

> the phrase ["feel themselves subdued"] ...has been interpreted and applied in more than one way... most jurists have interpreted it to apply to the People of the Book generally, when they enter into a treaty relationship with a Muslim state. *In Islamic history, some rulers have enforced a kind of humiliation to accompany the paying of the jizyah by the dhimmi communities*...[42,43]

---

[39] For an example of this friction see the "Universal Declaration", articles two and eight.
[40] My translation.
[41] Nasr et al., *The Study Quran*, 514.
[42] Caner K. Dagali, "Conquest and Conversion, War and Peace in the Quran," in *The Study Quran*, ed. Seyyed Hossein Nasr et al. (New York: HarperOne, 2015), 1811. (Emphasis added)
[43] It is important to note that Dagali goes on to write that the payment of *jizyah* with the additional feeling of humiliation "has generally gone against most established Islamic precedent and legal opinion". Dagli, "Conquest," 1811.

Mayer makes three points about the status of *dhimmis* in the Islamic state. First, that they were tolerated as long as they submitted to Muslim rule and accepted a number of conditions concerning their conduct. Second, although *dhimmis* were generally allowed to follow their own religious law, discriminatory practices existed in cases involving interactions between Muslims and *dhimmis*. Finally, Mayer notes that Muslims could not enter into treaties with polytheists and idolaters. This is because the latter two groups, at least in theory, were expected to embrace Islam or face death.[44] Again, verses such as 9:29 and the rulings derived therefrom can and have been interpreted differently. For example, Muslim traditionalists understand different religious forms as both necessary and providential. Therefore, they emphasize the Quranic principles of pluralism, inclusivity, and free will. Nevertheless, the issue of *dhimmis* in traditional Islamic law is clearly in conflict with modern human rights standards that maintain

> everyone is entitled to all the rights and freedoms set forth in this Declaration, without distinction of any kind, such as race, color, sex, language, religion, political or other opinion, national or social origin, property, birth or other status. Furthermore, no distinction shall be made on the basis of the political, jurisdictional or international status of the country or territory to which a person belongs, whether it be independent, trust, non-self-governing or under any other limitation of sovereignty.[45]

Finally, in the case of penal code, the main concern from a human rights perspective is Islamic law's use of corporeal punishment. For example, Katerina Dalacoura notes that many people would argue that the Quran's authoritative status "implies that...the *hadd* punishments can never be abandoned thereby creating a serious tension with international human rights principles"[46] Here, the term '*hadd*' refers to the concept of *ḥudūd Allah*, that is, the 'limits of God'. These limits are referred to throughout the Quran, and most Muslims generally consider them to be non-negotiable. In terms of corporeal punishment, six crimes fall under the rubric of the 'limits of God': theft, highway robbery, fornication, false accusations of fornication,

---

[44] Mayer, *Islam and Human Rights*, 135.
[45] "The Universal Declaration," article 2.
[46] Katerina Dalacoura, "Islam and Human Rights," in *The Essentials of Human Rights*, ed. Rhona Smith and Christien van den Anker (New York: Oxford University Press, 2005), 208.

intoxication, and apostasy.⁴⁷ The following two verses address the crimes of theft and adultery respectively:

> As for the thief, man or woman, cut off their hands as a requital for what they have earned. [That is] an exemplary punishment from Allah, and Allah is all-mighty, all-wise. (38) But whoever repents after his wrongdoing, and reforms, then Allah shall accept his repentance. Indeed Allah is all-forgiving, all-merciful. (5:38-39)

> As for the fornicatress and the fornicator, strike each of them a hundred lashes, and let not pity for them overcome you in Allah's law, if you believe in Allah and the Last Day, and let their punishment be witnessed by a group of the faithful. (24:2)

According to Abdullahi An-Na'im, "there is...no Qur'anic authority for abolishing the *hadud* in principle. What can be done from the Islamic point of view, is to restrict their application in practice."⁴⁸ Thus, the Quran's prescription of corporeal punishment seems to violate a number of international human rights laws. In particular, it seems to violate article five of the Universal Declaration which declares that, "No one shall be subjected to torture or to cruel, inhumane or degrading treatment or punishment."⁴⁹

How have Muslims responded to the existing tensions between Islamic law and international human rights law? The next section looks at contemporary Islamic thought and contemporary Muslim attempts at scriptural interpretation and legal reform in relation to human rights.

4.2. Understanding contemporary Islamic thought

The Muslim responses to the challenge of modernity and human rights is varied. They can be generally categorized into four broad groups: fundamentalist, liberal,

---

[47] Intoxication and apostasy are problematic because the Quran does not prescribe any specific worldly punishment for them. For example, An-Na'mi points out that "...The Qur'an does not prescribe any punishment for apostasy in this life. Nevertheless, the majority of Muslim jurists have classified apostasy as a *hadd* punishment punishable by death..." See An-Na'im, *Toward an Islamic Reformation: Civil Liberties, Human Rights and International Law* (New York: Syracuse University Press, 1990), 109.
[48] An-Na'im, *Towards an Islamic Reformation*, 108.
[49] "Universal Declaration," article five.

progressive, and traditionalist.[50] The so-called fundamentalist Muslims lie on one end of the spectrum. Their ideology is rooted in Salafism, which is derived from the word *salaf*, meaning the '[pious] ancestors'. Thus, they generally call for a return to an earlier and supposedly pristine form of Islam, and they reject the modern world as anti-religious, immoral, and imperialistic.[51] Most neo-Salafis do not get involved in politics; however, a minority believe in an offensive war against perceived threats to Islam.[52] The 'fundamentalist mentality', that is, the basic intellectual orientation of the *salafis*, follows in the footsteps of former modern revivalists such as Abul Alā Mawdūdī (d.1979), founder of Jamaat e-Islami and Sayyed Quṭb (d.1966), member of the Muslim Brotherhood. Maududi and Quṭb generally believed that Islam was a political force with the ability to govern a nation-state through the use of Islamic law or shariah. They insisted that all people have to make a fundamental choice between two competing and incompatible ideologies: (a revived) Islam or the 'West'. In this regard, for example, Sayyid Quṭb maintained that

> ...Sovereignty rests with God alone and...He is the Lord and Cherisher of the entire universe. This means that religion is an all-embracing and total revolution against the sovereignty of man in all its types, shapes, systems and states, and completely revolts against every system in which authority may be in the hands of man in any form or in other words, where he may have usurped sovereignty under any shape. Any system of governance in which the final decision is referred to human beings and they happen to be the source of all authority, in fact defies them by designating "others than God," as lords over men.[53]

---

[50] Of course, there is much overlap between these approaches and their advocates. This typology is simply meant to bring out the general trends in contemporary Islamic thought. Moreover, this section mainly focuses on the traditionalist and progressive schools for several reasons. First, an in-depth analysis of all major trends is beyond the scope of this work. Second, the traditionalist and progressive schools are the most nuanced and thorough in their respective approaches. Lastly, they also seem to be the most popular ideologies in the Western academic world concerning the subject of Islam and modernity.
[51] In general, see Bernard Haykel, "Salafis," in *The Princeton Encyclopedia of Islamic Thought*, ed. Bowering et al. (Princeton: Princeton University Press), 483-4.
[52] Haykel, "Salafis," 484.
[53] Sayyid Qutb, "War, Peace and Islamic Jihad," in *Modernist and Fundamentalist Debates in Islam: A Reader*, ed. Mansoor Moaddel and Kamran Talattof (New York: Palgrave, 2000), 228.

The problem with this approach lies in its extreme idealism, puritanism, and literalism. It dismisses much of Islam's 1400-years old intellectual and legal tradition as heretical innovation (*bid'ah*) and does not have the ability to respond to the constant changes of a temporal and relative world. Of course, there is nothing wrong with looking back at the time of the Prophet and his companions as a source for guidance; however, it is impossible to recreate the existent conditions of Arabian society in the seventh century.

On the other end of the spectrum are the so-called liberal Muslims. This work distinguishes them from progressive Muslims in so far as the former believe that Western civilization is always progressing and Muslims need to 'catch up'. This group gives little to no significance to their traditional heritage and advocates for a wholesale adoption of the modern mentality. Some of its members include populist authors, such as Irshad Manji, who generally have little to no formal education in traditional Islam. Manji, in her book – *The Trouble with Islam Today* – makes her stance clear. She writes,

> I have to be honest with you. Islam is on very thin ice with me.... Through our screaming self-pity and our conspicuous silences, we Muslims are conspiring against ourselves. We're in crisis and we're dragging the rest of the world with us. If ever there was a moment for an Islamic reformation, it's now.[54]

Therefore, liberal Muslims tend to agree with the dubious modern assumption that humankind is constantly progressing, and that this progress has culminated in the morality of the secular-liberal tradition today. As such, they generally believe that Islam should be reformed to conform to the moral standards of the day. The problem with this approach lies in its relative nature. If our standard of morality is derived from contemporary attitudes based on social laws and norms – and not a higher, transhistorical reality – then our understanding of right and wrong will always be in a state of flux. Moreover, our moral compass will always be open to manipulation by those in control over 'public information'. Omid Safi, a self-declared progressive Muslim, separates liberal and progressive Muslims by writing that, "...In our view, 'liberal Muslims' have been too eager to identify themselves wholeheartedly with European and American structures of power." Thus, "they have proven

---

[54] Irshad Manji, *The Trouble with Islam Today: A Wake-up Call for Honesty and Change* (Toronto: Random House Canada, 2003), 1-3.

unable and unwilling to adopt a critical stance against the injustices of *both* Muslims societies *and* Western hegemony."[55]

Progressive Muslims, on the other hand, define themselves as those united in the goal of establishing the concept that all human life has the same intrinsic worth and challenging oppressive practices in Western and Muslim societies – as well as those connected to globalization. In 1998, a number of progressive activists and scholars created a declaration called: Progressive Islam - A Definition and Declaration. In the declaration, they provided the following definition:

> Progressive Islam is that understanding of Islam and its sources which comes from and is shaped within a commitment to transform society from an unjust one where people are mere objects of exploitation by governments, socio-economic institutions and unequal relationships. The new society will be a just one where people are the subjects of history, the shapers of their own destiny in the full awareness that all of humankind is in a state of returning to God and that the universe was created as a sign of God's presence.[56]

Progressive Muslims adopt a number of methodologies in their attempts at reform; however, these methodologies are almost always fundamentally based on the twin concepts of contextuality and subjectivity.[57] In terms of contextuality, they point out that all developments in the Muslim world, including the revelation of the Quran, occurred at a particular time and place; therefore, some of these developments are absolute and universal and others are relative and contextual. Thus, progressive Muslims insist on reforming the Islamic tradition through contextual interpretation in line with the spirit of the Qur'an as a whole.[58] The crux of the problem is deciding the standard by which to separate the absolute from the relative or the spirit from the letter. For example, Abullahi An-Na'im, following in the footsteps of his teacher,

---

[55] Omid Safi, "Introduction: The Times are A-Changin' – A Muslim Quest for Justice, Gender Equality and Pluralism," in *Progressive Muslims: On Justice, Gender and Pluralism*, ed. Omid Safi (Oxford: Oneworld, 2003), 17.

[56] Farid Esack, "In Search of Progressive Islam Beyond 9/11," in *Progressive Muslims: On Justice, Gender and Pluralism*, ed. Omid Safi (Oxford: Oneworld, 2003), 80.

[57] Based on these approaches, progressive Muslims generally argue in favor of constitutional democracy and contemporary human rights; Moreover, they argue against hierarchical social and political structures, and any hegemonic interpretations of Islam.

[58] Progressive and traditionalist Muslims agree on this point. However, they differ when it comes to their approaches and conclusions.

argues that the verses revealed in Medina were specifically intended for the Muslims at that time. They provided guidance on how to construct a new community within the context of seventh-century Arabia. Thus, for An- Na'im, verses about inheritance, divorce, and the like are no longer applicable today. As such, it is only the verses that were revealed in Mecca that are universal and apply to all Muslims in all places and at all times.[59] Thus, An- Na'im attempts to create a new foundation for Islamic law based on the legal concept of abrogation. In this regard, he writes:

> The basic premise of *Ustadh* Mahmoud is that a close examination of the content of the Quran and Sunna reveals two levels or stages of the message of Islam, one of the earlier Mecca period and the other of the subsequent Medina stage. Furthermore, he maintained that the earlier message of Mecca is in fact the eternal and fundamental message of Islam… [Therefore, when the Meccan message] was violently and irrationally rejected…the more realistic message of the Medina stage was provided… [Hence,] aspects of the Mecca message…were postponed for implementation under appropriate circumstances in the future.[60]

To give another example of the contextual approach, Abdolkarim Soroush argues that it is an epistemological truth that texts cannot stand alone; this is because texts are understood by humans, and the latter are conditioned and contained within their societies' parameters of knowledge. Thus, the understandings of texts are framed and determined by human collectivities. In this regard, Soroush writes:

> …one can say that the text does not stand alone, it does not carry its own meaning on its shoulders, it needs to be situated in a context, it is theory-laden, its interpretation is in flux, and presumptions are at work here as elsewhere in the field of understanding. Religious texts are no exception. Therefore, their interpretation is subject to expansion and contraction according to the assumptions preceding them and/or the questions enquiring them.[61]

For Soroush, this means that religious knowledge is strictly a human science; therefore, its 'prior text' should be based on substantiated theories of the

---

[59] In general, see An-Na'im, *Toward an Islamic Reformation*.
[60] An-Na'im, *Toward an Islamic Reformation*, 52-3.
[61] Abdolkarim Soroush, "The Evolution and Devolution of Religious Knowledge," in *Liberal Islam: A Sourcebook* ed. Charles Kruzman (New York: Oxford University Press, 1998), 245.

present time. According to him, it is only when this happens that Muslims can embrace democracy and the plurality of religions.[62] Thus, Soroush's litmus test for separating the relative from the absolute is substantiated (but relative) theories of the time, and An-Na'im's test is the distinction between Meccan and Medinian verses.

Along with context, many progressive Muslims also insist on the concept of subjectivity, that is, the idea that all reality is filtered through a subject and therefore colored by that subject's particularities. In other words, they argue that humans cannot know the truth as such; they can only know it as they see it, that is, through the lens of their socio-economic, racial, ethnic and gendered identities. In this regard, for example, Amina Wadud aptly titles her work, *Quran and Woman: Rereading the Sacred Text from a Women's Perspective*. In her methodological attempt to pursue a female inclusive reading of the Quran, Wadud writes:

> …In these times of postmodernist critique when the very foundations of knowledge are challenged to move beyond certain value laden tendencies, such a method can be viewed as part of a larger area of discourse by feminists who have constructed a valuable critique of the tendency in many disciplines to build the notion of the normative human from the experiences and perspectives of the male person.[63]

More explicitly, Wadud writes that her text "contributes to the post-colonial, postmodern field of Islamic studies by its focus on gender as a category of thought — not just a subject for discourse."[64] To provide a final example on subjectivity, Sa'diyya Shaikh approaches the subject of reforming Islamic law by exploring the latter's underlying worldview, principles, and norms. She argues that this approach is necessary because it questions the metaphysical foundations of the shariah itself. In this regard she argues that the Islamic mystical tradition, and the famous Andalusian mystic, ibn 'Arabī, provide rich spaces of divergence that can be used to challenge Islamic thought and its concomitant gender laws. However, whenever ibn 'Arabī's views contradict Shaikh's understanding and goals, she is forced to revert back to the popular progressive approach based on subjectivity. Thus, in discussing ibn 'Arabī's

---

[62] Soroush, "Evolution and Devolution."
[63] Amina Wadud, *Qur'an and Woman: Rereading the Sacred Text from a Women's Perspective* (New York: Oxford University Press, 1999), ix.
[64] Wadud, *Qur'an and Woman*, xi.

notion of masculinity in relation to prophecy, for example, she writes in presumptuous and dismissive fashion:

> A feminist musing by an Ibn Arabi enthusiast might present the view that perhaps he was deliberately affirming his patriarchal audience's symbolic and psychological needs while presenting them with some unpalatable positions regarding women's actual complete spiritual equality that were almost heretically gender egalitarian. *Or perhaps he was simply limited by his own subjectivity, which was always also enmeshed within a patriarchal symbolic universe.*[65]

The twin concepts of contextuality and subjectivity are highlighted by the progressive Muslim's emphasis on the importance of separating Divine law (shariah) from Islamic jurisprudence (*fiqh*). In doing so, they emphasize the difference between sacred law revealed by God, and its understanding and development constructed by humans. This idea opens the door to new and different interpretations, and the possibility of legal reform. In any case, the considerations of contextuality and subjectivity are not alien to the Islamic intellectual tradition. For example, in terms of contextuality, premodern Muslim scholars have written on the subject of the occasions or reasons for revelation *(asbāb al-nuzūl)*. Nevertheless, according to the Islamic intellectual tradition, the context of a verse, however important, can never exhaust its meaning. This explains the astounding number of commentaries which have been written on the Quran and each of its verses. Premodern Muslim scholars have also acknowledged the concept of human subjectivity and its limits on human knowledge. For example, this is seen in the works of many legal texts where religious rulings are commonly followed by phrases such as, "And God knows best." Moreover, the idea that God knows better than His creation is constantly emphasized in the Quran.[66] Despite this however, the Islamic intellectual tradition has always balanced the concept of subjectivity with the concept of transcendence and the respective possibility of objectivity.[67] Therefore, Muslim traditionalists insist that there are *degrees* of knowledge which increase according to one's spiritual state. For example, in terms of knowledge and objectivity, Schuon writes that "Man is intelligence, and intelligence is the transcending of forms and the realization of the invisible

---

[65] Saʿdiyya Shaikh, *Sufi Narratives of Intimacy: Ibn ʿArabi, Gender and Sexuality* (Chapel Hill: The University of North Carolina Press, 2012), 90.
[66] For a small sample size, see verses 3:36, 3:167, 84:23, and 21:40.
[67] For a thorough treatment of Perennialism's perspective on transcendence, knowledge, and objectivity, see Schuon, *Logic and Transcendence*.

Essence; to say human intelligence is to say absoluteness and transcendence." [68] In short, one of the major problems with the progressive school is its almost exclusive reliance on the socio-historical method, and its tendency to dismiss or negate what many Muslims consider sacred, such as the hadith literature or the shariah as a whole. For example, An- Na'im's suggestion of abrogating verses revealed in Medina seems untenable since Muslims consider the entirety of the Quran as the verbatim and universal speech of God. Moreover, the dismissal of 'objective knowledge' can be equated with the dismissal of the purpose of religion and life itself: the spiritual movement from the temporal self towards the Absolute Reality.[69]

In any case, the current climate of islamophpobia and globalization seem to be pushing Muslims towards the extremes of liberalism or fundamentalism. This is because an aggressive attitude towards any single group of people will always force the latter to either 'give in' or 'dig in'. Nevertheless, these two groups make up a small minority of the Muslim population. Most Muslims place themselves somewhere in-between these two extremes. It seems that the progressive approach is the most popular among Muslims working in Western academic institutions.[70] Nevertheless, my working assumption is that many Muslims continue to understand their religion through traditional forms; therefore, they are most closely represented by the perennial school of thought in the Islamic context, that is, Islamic traditionalism. As mentioned, this is one of the reasons why I am using this school as a framework for my theory of virtue ethics. In doing so, I am attempting to approach Muslims as equal agents that possess self-understanding and have the right to self-determination. In any case, in order to provide the necessary context, the next section of this chapter situates the perennial school of thought – both historically and thematically – within the larger field of religious studies.[71]

4.3. The perennial school of thought and Islamic traditionalism

By the twentieth century, Western peoples found themselves living in a new world that was based on the ideals of secular-liberalism and functioned within the social institutions of democracy, capitalism, standardized education, and

---

[68] Frithjof Schuon, *The Transfiguration of Man* (Bloomington: World Wisdom, 1995), 24.
[69] In other words, progressive Muslims have a tendency to reduce Islam to an ideology concerned with social justice and, in doing so, they bypass issues of truth and spirituality.
[70] This includes academics such as, Abdullahi An-Nai'm, Sa'diyya Shaikh, Amina Wadud, Abdulaziz Sachedina and Khalid Abou El Fadl.
[71] As mentioned, Islamic traditionalism is the perennial school of thought applied within the Islamic context.

the like.[72] A number of changes coalesced to produce this transition. These included the Renaissance; the Scientific and Industrial Revolutions; the independence of France and America; the Age of Enlightenment; and the rise of Protestantism.[73] These were revolutionary periods that transformed the human being's understanding of the self and the world. For example, the scientific and industrial revolutions were largely responsible for the popular belief in human progress independent of revelation and religion. In this regard, Huston Smith writes:

> ...Progress [is] the hope that has powered the modern world... To set that hope in perspective we need only go back to Revolution of Rising Expectations that the Scientific and Industrial Revolutions gave rise to. Hegel cashed in on the forward-looking stance of those revolutions and fashioned from it a worldview. From the seeming fact that things *were* getting better and stood a good chance of continuing to doing so, Hegel extrapolated backward to infer that they had *always* been improving...Support for this heady scenario was welcomed from every quarter...[74,75]

In any case, these changes resulted in backlash from some members of society. In the twentieth century, a particularly strong reaction came from what would become known as the perennial school of thought. For members of this school, the deterioration of older institutions was the symptom of a much larger problem: the modern mentality and its virtual dismissal of the eternal truths of religion which were expressed in almost all premodern societies, albeit in different ways and to different degrees. In other words, they

---

[72] Huston Smith divides the history of Western peoples into four major periods that are differentiated by their basic assumptions and ways of 'understanding the world'. These are: the Graeco-Roman or Classical age; European Christendom; the Scientific or Modern period; and the Postmodern age. See Huston Smith, *Beyond the Postmodern Mind: The Place of Meaning in a Global Civilization*, 3rd ed. (Illinois: Quest Books, 2003), 3-16.

[73] More specifically, within these defining periods there were monumental inventions and developments, such as the invention of the printing press and growth of popular literacy.

[74] Huston Smith, *Why Religion Matters: The Fate of The Human Spirit in an Age of Disbelief* (New York: HarperOne, 2001), 150.

[75] It is important to note that perennialists object to scientism and not science as such. The former is the belief that science is the only method for obtaining objective truth because it deals with the most fundamental elements of existence. See Smith, *Why Religion Matters*, 59-60.

argued that the new ways in which we understood ourselves and the world was fundamentally flawed and opposed the perennial wisdom of the ages. For example, according to Guenon:

> A word that rose to honor at the time of the Renaissance, and that summarized in advance the whole program of modern civilization is 'humanism'. Men were indeed concerned to reduce everything to purely human proportions, to eliminate every principle of a higher order, and, one might say, symbolically to turn away from the heavens under pretext of conquering the earth... Humanism was the first form of what has subsequently become contemporary secularism; and, owing to its desire to reduce everything to the measure of man as an end in himself, modern civilization has sunk stage by stage until it has reached the level of the lowest elements in man and aims at little more than satisfying the needs inherent in the material side of his nature...[76]

Thus, perennialists oppose the modern mentality on a whole, that is, all the ideologies that underlie modern societies. These ideologies can be grouped under the umbrella of humanism and they include, among others, liberalism, individualism, historicism, rationalism, and scientism. However, for perennialists, the 'modern age' is also an inevitable period in the unfolding of world history. This is because it is the period that every major religion has foreseen and warned against: the 'latter days' that precede the 'end of the world'.[77] In this regard, Lings wrote:

> ...The tradition of the four ages of the cycle of time which the Greeks and Romans named the Golden, Silver, Bronze and Iron Ages, is not merely European but is also to be found in Asia, among the Hindus, and in America among the Red Indians. According to Hinduism, which has the most explicit doctrine on the subject, the Golden Age was by far the longest; the ages became increasingly shorter as they were less good, the shortest and worst being the dark age, which corresponds to the Iron Age... The same truth, clothed in many different imageries, has come down to us out of the prehistoric past in all parts of the

---

[76] Rene Guenon, *The Crisis of the Modern World*, 4th ed., trans. Arthur Osborne, Marco Pallis and Richard C. Nicholson (Bloomington: Sophia Perennis, 2001), 17.
[77] In general, see Charles Upton, *Legends of the End: Prophecies of the End Times, Antichrist, Apocalypse, and Messiah from Eight Religious Traditions* (New York: Sophia Perennis, 2005).

world. Religions are in fact unanimous in teaching not evolution but devolution.[78]

Thus, in light of religious eschatological doctrines, perennialists do not perceive themselves as socio-political reformers.[79,80] Rather, they are primarily concerned with what is commonly referred to as the 'perennial philosophy'.[81] According to Clinton Minnaar, the perennial philosophy is

> ... both absolute Truth and infinite Presence. As absolute Truth it is the perennial wisdom (*sophia perennis*) that stands as the transcendent source of all the intrinsically orthodox religions of humankind. In the words of St. Augustine, it is that "uncreated Wisdom, the same now, as before, and the same to be forevermore" ... As infinite Presence it is the perennial religion (*religio perennis*) that lives within the heart of all intrinsically orthodox religions. In the words of Cardinal Nicholas of Cusa: "There is...one sole religion and one sole worship for all beings endowed with understanding, and this is presupposed through a variety of rites..."[82]

Thus, the perennial philosophy maintains that virtually all of the world's religions contain the same metaphysical truths and that differences are a matter of formal expressions and areas of emphasis. Moreover, perennialists believe that existence of different religions is providential because it provides a number of paths that allow human beings to return to God. Thus, the

---

[78] Martin Lings, "The Past in the Light of the Present and The Rhythms of Time," in *The Underlying Religion: An Introduction to the Perennial Philosophy*, ed. Martin Lings and Clinton Minnaar (Bloomington: World Wisdom, 2006), 36-7.

[79] There are a few groups that believe the 'perennial philosophy' should be used towards socio-political ends. For a historical treatment of perennialism and an account of these groups, see Mark Sedgwick, *Against the Modern World: Traditionalism and the Secret Intellectual History of the Twentieth Century* (Oxford: Oxford University Press, 2004).

[80] In line with the perennialist school, my work is not primarily an attempt to facilitate any type of socio-political reform. Rather, it is an attempt to critically explore human rights and its level of compatibility with the Quranic worldview and Islamic intellectual tradition.

[81] The perennial philosophy is also commonly referred to as 'traditionalism'. As mentioned in the introduction, the term 'tradition' implies both the revelation of truth and the unfolding of that truth within particular societies.

[82] Clinton Minnaar, "Introduction," in *The Underlying Religion: An Introduction to the Perennial Philosophy*, ed. Martin Lings and Clinton Minnaar (Bloomington: World Wisdom, 2006), xii

perennial philosophy is not a syncretic philosophy. This is why Minnaar goes on to write:

> … it is precisely this "sole religion" that Frithjof Schuon has called the "underlying religion" or "religion of the heart" … which is the heart of all religion. It should be clearly understood, however, that the "underlying religion" is of an essentially supra-formal, universal, or spiritual nature. Although it resides as an immanent and underlying presence within the religions, it is not itself a formal or particular religion… In other words, the "underlying religion" remains transcendent vis-à-vis the religions, even while being a vivifying presence within them. It is no way a "new religion". [83]

Thus, perennialism is a school of comparative religion that is based on the perennial philosophy. It argues that all religions contain the same metaphysical truths; explains how these truths were expressed in premodern societies; and uses the perennial philosophy to judge and critique the modern worldview and its underlying ideologies.[84] This unique approach to religion found its most thorough expression in Frithjof Schuon's work, *The Transcendent Unity of Religions*.[85] In order to understand his work, it is important to put it in context with other approaches to the study of religion.

Premodern education was generally oral, interactive, holistic, and religious in nature. It also had a common ideal: maintaining a structured society based on the 'nature of things'. The idea was simple: living according to the 'laws of heaven' would ensure an orderly and peaceful individual, family, and society.[86] Therefore, the teachers or elders were responsible for passing down sacred laws and customs, and the latter were generally enshrined within a particular cultural tradition's folklore.[87] The interconnection between the student and their object of study was most apparent in the area of religion.

---

[83] Minnaar, "Introduction," xii-xiii

[84] These 'expressions' include everything from metaphysical and cosmological doctrines, to scared mythology and art.

[85] Schuon Frithjof, *The Transcendent Unity of Religions*, 2nd ed. (Illinois: Quest Books, 1993).

[86] Of course, this is an overgeneralization. For a more nuanced approach to premodern education, see John Hinnells, ed., *The Routledge Companion to The Study of Religion* (New York: Routledge, 2010). Also see Jane Casewit, ed., *Education in the Light of Tradition: Studies in Comparative Religion* (Bloomington: World Wisdom Inc., 2011).

[87] Eric J. Sharpe, "The Study of Religion in Historical Perspective," in *The Routledge Companion to the Study of Religion*, ed. John Hinnells (New York: Routledge, 2010), 22-3.

That is to say, students of religion were also religious students, and a large part of their learning included the practice of sacred rites and rituals.[88] They did not 'objectively' study religion from a 'detached' sociological, psychological, or historical perspective. They were primarily interested in the truth, and a student's level of knowledge, or stage of education, was largely determined by their spiritual state and moral character. In this sense, it can be argued that every member of society was a student of religion. Moreover, in premodern societies, it would be misleading to separate religion from other disciplines of study. This is because, in one sense, it was the only subject; it unified and directed all other disciplines. In doing so, it made them religious and gave them their significance. However, by the twentieth century, education had drastically changed. The subject of religion, like all others, was cut off from any overarching and sacred principles. Across Western universities, the theological study of religion was, by and large, replaced by the academic study of religion.[89] This transformation is commonly associated with Max Muller (d.1900) who believed that religion had governing principles, and that these principles could be discovered through the objective and methodic collection of data. This was a direct consequence of the rise and influence of scientific positivism in society in general, and in education in particular. The goal was to seek "out those elements, patterns, and principles that could be found uniformly in the religions of all times and places."[90] The academic study of religion sought to answer two main questions: the origin and function of religion. Here, the 'origin' didn't refer to a transcendental and primordial moment of creation; rather, it referred to religions' human origin in so far as people organized into religious groups for a number of social ends.[91] In attempting to answer these two questions, the academic study of religion became highly interdisciplinary and specialized; this resulted in a number of different approaches with their own prior assumptions and conclusions.

The modern approaches to religion can be divided and categorized in many ways.[92] The first and initial division was between the theological study of religion and the academic study of religion. The former preserved the concept

---

[88] Sharpe, "Study of Religion," 24.
[89] Sharpe, "The Study of Religion," 21-38.
90 Daniel L. Pals, *Nine Theories of Religion*, 3rd ed. (Oxford: Oxford University Press, 2015), 1-2.
[91] Robert A. Segal, "Theories of Religion," in *The Routledge Companion to the Study of Religion*, ed. John Hinnells (New York: Routlege, 2010), 75-76.
[92] I have mainly relied on two sources for my particular categorization. These are Hinnells, ed., *Routledge Companion* and Huston Smith, "Introduction" to *The Transcendent Unity* by Frithjof Schuon, 2nd ed. (Illinois: Quest Books, 1993), ix-xxxvii.

of objective truth – a concept central to every religious tradition. In doing so however, it abandoned the 'impartial' stance that had become necessary for scholarly research. Thus, in Western academies, the academic study of religion and its numerous approaches dominated the field of religious studies. Within this second group there was a further division between the nominalists and the essentialists. The latter, who are more central to the aims of this work, were again divided into two groups: the reductionists and the phenomenologists.[93] The reductionists maintained that the origin and function of religion can be reduced to a non-religious and worldly phenomenon. Most famously, Freud reduced religion to psychology, Marx reduced it to economics, and Durkheim reduced it to sociology. For example, Freud argued that God, and by extension religion, originated and functioned to fill the psychological need that humans have for explanation and comfort – a need that a father would normally provide for his child. In this light, Freud wrote:

> If one wishes to form a true estimate of the full grandeur of religion, one must keep in mind what it undertakes to do for men. It gives them information about the source and origin of the universe, it assures them of protection and final happiness amid the changing vicissitudes of life, and it guides their thoughts and emotions by means of precepts which are backed by the whole force of its authority.[94]

The phenomenologists, on the other hand, argued that humans were religious by nature, and they wanted to 'let religion speak for itself'. For them, arguing that religion was something other than religion was explaining away the phenomena that the reductionists were trying to explain.[95] In order to keep the religious nature of religion intact, phenomenologists searched for a common origin and function of religions that was also religious in nature. Thus, for example, Rudolph Otto (d.1937) argued that the heart of religion was an experience of the numinous;[96] Friedrich Schleiermacher (d.1834) argued

---

[93] Smith, "Introduction."
[94] Sigmund. Freud, "Lecture XXXV: A Philosophy of Life," Marxist Internet Archive, accessed June 14, 2017, https://www.marxists.org/reference/subject/philosophy/works/at/freud.htm.
[95] Pals, *Nine Theories*, 230-1.
[96] See Rudolph Otto, *The Idea of the Holy an Inquiry into the Non-Rational Factor in the Idea of the Divine and its Relation to the Rational*, 2nd ed., trans. John W. Harvey (New York: Oxford University Press, 1950).

that it was an intuition or feeling of dependence;[97] and Mircea Eliade (d.1986) argued that it was in the dichotomy that humans create between the sacred and the profane.[98] Eliade readily admitted that religion involves "the social man, the economic man, and so forth"; however, he insisted that "all these conditioning factors together do not, of themselves, add up to the life of the spirit."[99] However, for the phenomenologists, the essence or origin of religion always fell on the human side of the God/human divide because studying phenomena meant putting aside metaphysical considerations. According to Smith, both approaches to religion, that is, the theological and phenomenological, are problematic. This is because the phenomenological approach is unbiased; however, it is unable to escape the subject's relative experiences. On the other hand, the theological approach preserves the concept of truth; however, it is biased because it is forced to favor one religion over another. In this regard, Smith succinctly explains the problem by stating that

> The two positions, theological and phenomenological, pull in opposite directions… So one could predict even before looking that efforts would be made to close the gap, to contrive a *via media* that retains the virtues of both positions (commitment and fair play) while eliminating their defects (prejudice and relativism). One can also see a priori the formal conditions a middle way must satisfy. First, it must center in something the great traditions have in common. But second, this something must be God-ward of the God/man divide, for attitudes, sentiments, and experiences, however lofty, are only human states and do not elicit worship.[100]

This problem was addressed by Schuon and his articulation of the perennial school's approach to the study of religion. For Schuon, the origin and essence of religion is metaphysical and transcendent. It lies at the apex of the esoteric, that is, the First Principle or the Divine Absolute. In other words, religions are ultimately one *in divinnis*. However, they become increasingly 'different' as

---

[97] See Karl Barth, *The Theology of Schleiermacher*, trans. Geoffrey Bromiley (Michigan: Eerdmans, 1982).
[98] See Mircea Eliade, *Images and Symbols: Studies in Religious Symbolism*, trans. Philip Mairet (New Jersey: Princeton University Press, 1991).
[99] Eliade, *Images and Symbols*, 32.
[100] Smith, "Introduction," xxii.

they descend towards the exoteric plane.[101] This is because on the exoteric plane, metaphysical truth is expressed by way of forms, and these forms are, by definition, exclusive to one another. Ultimately, this means that religions have an 'underlying unity' and function as 'paths that lead to the same summit'. In this way, Schuon kept the Divine origin of religion intact, without being biased towards one particular religious path. However, the issue that his approach presents is that it is supra-formal; in other words, on the formal or worldly plane, it is clear that religions are different and within each religion, there are significant religious differences. Thus, the unity of religions – contained in the knowledge of the Absolute – is not simply observed or rationalized; rather, it is perceived by the Intellect and best explained by way of sacred symbols and mythology. Here, we come to an important point in the perennial school's epistemology. For perennialists, this type of knowledge proceeds from the Intellect – that is, the part of the human being that understands reality intuitively, certainly, and immediately. In terms of the Intellect, Lings explains the following:

> The meeting point of the two natures [that is, the Divine and human], the summit of the soul which is also its center…is what most religions name the Heart…and the Heart is the throne of the Intellect in the sense in which *Intellectus* was used throughout the middle ages, that is, the "solar" faculty which perceives spiritual truths directly unlike the "lunar" faculties of reason, memory and imagination, which are the differentiated reflections of the Intellect.[102, 103]

Thus, the Intellect, by way of 'intellection' or 'intellectual intuition', is the faculty that is able to know reality and distinguish the absolute from the relative. According to Nasr,

---

[101] According to the perennial school, the transcendent unity of religions does not lead to the negation of different religious forms on the worldly plane. On the contrary, religious pluralism is understood as both necessary and providential.

[102] Lings, "Past in Light," 51.

[103] The faculty that is able to possess this particular type of knowledge is hereon referred to as the Intellect or the Heart. Strictly speaking, these two faculties are not the identical with one another; however, their differences are inconsequential to the aims of this book and, therefore, they are used synonymously in the following chapters. Moreover, the Intellect and the Heart have been capitalized in order to distinguish them from their commonplace usage as a mental faculty and an emotional sense respectively.

> *Scientia sacra* is none other than that sacred knowledge which lies at the heart of every revelation and is the center of that circle which encompasses and defines tradition. The first question… [is] how is the attainment of such a knowledge possible? The answer of tradition is that the twin source of this knowledge is revelation and intellection, or intellectual intuition which involves the illumination of the heart and the mind of man and the presence in him of knowledge of an immediate and direct nature which is tasted and experienced…[104]

On the other hand, the mind is the faculty that is responsible for reasoning, classifying, explaining, and the like. On this view, the perennial school maintains that reason can be tied to the Intellect and therefore rooted in the transcendent, or it can be tied to the passions and therefore rooted in the relative.[105] Moreover, this supra-formal Intellectual knowledge has two principal sources: The already mentioned Intellect and, second, the different forms of Divine revelation found within the worlds religious traditions such as the Hindu Vedas, Christian Bible, and the Islamic Quran. For this reason, perennialists generally take a stand against ideologies that overemphasize the concepts of 'contextuality' and 'subjectivity' in order to reform religion. It is not because these existential limitations do not exist; rather, it is because they exist on some levels and to some degrees. In any case, it is in light of the Intellect's direct perception of Divine unity that perennialism explains the ways in which the Divine reveals or expresses itself – through different religions – in the formal realm. Schuon illustrates this invoking the symbolism of light:

> If an example may be drawn from the sensory sphere to illustrate the difference between metaphysical and theological knowledge, it may be said that the former, which can be called 'esoteric' when it is manifested though a religious symbolism, is conscious of the colourless essence of light and of its character of pure luminosity; a given religious belief, on the other hand, will assert that light is red and

---

[104] S. H. Nasr, "Scientia Sacra," in *The Underlying Religion: An Introduction to the Perennial Philosophy*, ed. Martin Lings and Clinton Minnaar (Bloomington: World Wisdom, 2006), 114.

[105] Frithjof Schuon, "The Primacy of Intellection," *Studies in Comparative Religion* 16, no. 3 and 4 (Summer-Autumn 1984), http://www.studiesincomparativereligion.com/public/articles/the_primacy_of_intellection-by_frithjof_schuon.aspx. Also see Rene Guenon, "Oriental Metaphysics," in *The Sword of Gnosis: Metaphysics, Cosmology, Tradition, Symbolism*, ed. Jacob Needleman (Baltimore: Penguin Books, 1974), 40-57.

not green, whereas another belief will assert the opposite; both will be right insofar as they distinguish light from darkness but no insofar as they identify it with a particular colour. This very rudimentary example is designed to show that the theological point of view, because it is based in the mind of believers on a Revelation and not on a knowledge that is accessible to each one of them…will of necessity confuse the symbol or form with the names and supra formal Truth, while the metaphysic, …will be able to make use of the same symbol or form as a means of expression while at the same time being aware of its relativity. That is why each of the great and intrinsically orthodox religions can…serve as a means of expression for every truth known directly by the eye of the Intellect …[106]

To provide a more concrete example, according to the perennial school, the idea of the *logos*, that is, 'the Word', can be found – on an esoteric level – in virtually all religious traditions. For example, in Christianity, God uses the pure vessel of the 'virgin' Mary to reveal 'the Word', that is, Christ, in order to give the faithful a path to return back to God. In the Bible, Christ is reported as saying, "none shall arrive at the Father, except through me." [107, 108] In Islam, God uses the pure vessel of the 'unlettered' Prophet to reveal 'the Word', that is, the Quran, in order to give the faithful a different but equally Divine path to return to God. It is reported that the Prophet said, "Truly, I am leaving behind amongst you two weighty things…the book of God and the People of my House (*Ahl al-Bayt*), they will not be parted from each other until they return to me at…*al-hawd*"[109] Thus, on the esoteric level, Christ and the Quran are two forms or embodiments for the same essence, that is, the incarnate 'Word of God', and it is through the latter that humans beings can return to their primordial and Divine origin.[110,111]

---

[106] Schuon, *Transcendent Unity*, xxx-xxxi.

[107] As quoted in William Stoddart, "Mysticism," in *The Underlying Religion: An Introduction to the Perennial Philosophy*, ed. Martin Lings and Clinton Minnaar (Bloomington: World Wisdom, 2006), 237.

[108] On the exoteric plane, the term 'me' refers to the figure of Christ; however, on the esoteric plane, the term 'me' refers to the *logos*, that is, 'the Word of God' found in every religion.

[109] As quoted in: Shah-Kazemi, *Justice and Remembrance*, 17.

[110] For an explanation of the function of the *Logos* in religion, see Stoddart, "Mysticism," 230-42.

Islamic traditionalism is the perennial school's particular explanation of the Islamic intellectual tradition in light of the perennial truths found in all religions. More specifically, Muslim traditionalists are concerned with the perennial truths contained in the Quran and the different ways that they have been understood and expressed by Muslims and Muslim societies throughout Islamic history. According to Chittick, they are concerned with "...the ways of thinking about God, the world, and the human being established by the Qur'ān and the Prophet and elaborated upon generations of practicing Muslims"[112] According to Muslim traditionalists, this involves a remarkable plurality that is held together by an underlying unity. In this regard, Nasr writes:

> In the vast world of Islam also, one can gain a better grasp of the whole by separating the patterns and seeing how each is related to vertical and horizontal dimensions of Islam itself as well as to cultural, ethnic, and linguistic factors. Then reuniting the patterns and seeing how they all fit together yields a vision of the total spectrum of Islam, in which unity leads to diversity and diversity is integrated into unity.[113]

He goes on to mention that some of the general factors that create unity between Muslims across spacio-temporal boundaries are the Quran, Sunna, and hadith in general, and the belief in Divine unity, prophecy, and eschatology in particular.[114] Moreover, on the human plane, Nasr points to the remarkable integration of plurality into unity when it comes to the shariah's religious rites, the Islamic mystical tradition, and all forms of Islamic art.[115,116]

---

[111] This fundamental concept is also seen in Hinduism where Krishna uses the pure vessel of the 'flute' to reveal 'the Word', that is, play music, and cause his followers to leave the world and return to him dancing. In this regard, see David R. Kinsley, *The Sword and the Flute: Kali and Krishna: Dark Visions of the Terrible and the Sublime in Hindu Mythology* (California: University of California Press, 1975).

[112] William Chittick, "Can the Islamic Intellectual Heritage be Recovered?," Iqbal Academy Pakistan, accessed December 7, 2017, http://www.allamaiqbal.com/publica tions/journals/review/oct98/2.htm#:~:text=No%20recovery%20of%20the%20intellectu al,through%20their%20own%2C%20personal%20ta%D8%A1q%C4%ABq.

[113] Nasr, *Heart of Islam*, 57.

[114] Of course, these Islamic sources have been interpreted differently, and they have given rise to different schools of thought. Nevertheless, these interpretations are rooted in the Quran and hadith; therefore, they are accepted as part and parcel of the diverse but unified Islamic civilization.

[115] Nasr, *Heart of Islam*, 58-9.

[116] For example, in terms of the underlying unity of Islamic art, see Titus Burckhardt, *Art of Islam: Language and Meaning* (Bloomington: World Wisdom, 2009).

More concretely, Nasr explains that Islamic traditionalism embraces all of traditional Islam, that is, Islam as it began from the time of Prophet until the dawn of the modern era. In doing so, it accepts the Quran as the sacred and verbatim word of God; the Sunni and Shiah hadith corpuses; the shariah and its historical development; and the Islamic intellectual tradition, that is, virtually all the different schools of Islamic theological, philosophical, and mystical thought.[117] In terms of the latter, Muslim traditionalists understand and accept the vast differences of opinion among premodern Muslim scholars. However, they understand these differences as rooted in the Quran, and, therefore, authentic manifestations of the Islamic revelation and its worldview. Ultimately, the school of Islamic traditionalism argues that Islam is a single and unified religious tradition with numerous and valid expressions.

This book argues that Islamic traditionalism's 'perennial standard' serves as an adequate litmus test by which to separate the Quran's absolute principals from their relative applications and expressions. The basic assumption of this standard is that any idea that is found in all religious traditions, which have existed for centuries across different spacio-temporal contexts, is ahistorical and, therefore, absolute and eternal. Moreover, the 'perennial standard' has its basis in the Quran and its conceptions of religious pluralism (*ahl al-kitāb*), Absolute Truth (*al-Haqq*), the primordial religion (*dīn al-qayyim*), and the innate human state (*fiṭrah*). To provide one example, in the case of religious pluralism, the Quran reads:

> … For each [community] among you We had appointed a code [of law] and a path, and had Allah wished He would have made you one community, but [His purposes required] that He should test you in respect to what He has given you. So take the lead in all good works. To Allah shall be the return of you all, whereat He will inform you concerning that about which you used to differ. (5:48)

> Indeed the faithful, the Jews, the Christians and the Sabaeans—those of them who have faith in Allah and the Last Day and act righteously—they shall have their reward from their Lord, and they will have no fear, nor will they grieve. (2:62)

> O mankind! Indeed, We created you from a male and a female, and made you nations and tribes that you may identify yourselves with one

---

[117] Nasr, *Islam in the Modern World*, 4-6.

another. Indeed the noblest of you in the sight of Allah is the most Godwary among you. Indeed Allah is all-knowing, all-aware. (49:13)

In addition to having its basis in the Quran, Islamic traditionalism has the advantage of approaching Islam holistically, working from within the Islamic tradition, and accepting Muslims as agents with self-understanding and the right to determine and pursue their own vision of 'the good'. Thus, the 'perennial standard' is the interpretive methodology that I apply in the following chapters – it informs the choices and interpretations of the sources I use. Here, it is important to note that the Quran was revealed in a specific context and many of its verses were revealed in response to particular situations. However, any objection to this work based on the 'occasions of revelation' misses the point. This is because this work is concerned with the ways in which the Quran and hadith contributed to the creation of the Muslim intellectual and ethical ethos, which is still very much alive today. With this in mind, I formulate my theory of virtue ethics by drawing on the work of Muslim traditionalists, as well as the two primary sources of the Quran and the thought of Imam Ali.

Chapter 5

Traditional Islamic Ethics and the Concept of Virtue

Elizabeth Ann Mayer prefaces her book on Islam and human rights by writing the following:

> This study focuses on the legal dimensions of human rights problems, examining the questions within the framework of comparative law and comparative legal history. Given the centrality of law in the Islamic tradition, the legal emphasis is warranted. However, there is no intention to imply that Islam is exclusively a legal tradition or that comparative legal history is the only legitimate way to approach the topic. In a more comprehensive study on the relationship of Islamic to human rights, one would ideally want to include analysis of how principles of Islamic theology, philosophy and ethics tie in with the treatment of human rights… This would carry one into areas beyond the comparative legal analysis of civil and political rights that is the sole concern of this study.[1]

These types of studies, which focus solely on Islamic law, are deeply problematic. This is because the Islamic legal tradition is grounded in the general Islamic worldview which is most clearly articulated by the Islamic intellectual tradition as a whole. According to Smith:

> The dominant assumptions of an age color the thoughts, beliefs, expectations, and images of the men and women who live within it. Being always with us, these assumptions usually pass unnoticed… But this doesn't mean they have no effect. Ultimately, assumptions which underlie our outlooks on life refract the world in ways that condition our art and our institutions…our sense of right and wrong, our criteria of success, what we conceive our duty to be [and so on.][2]

---

[1] Mayer, *Islam and Human Rights*, xvii.
[2] Smith, *Beyond the Postmodern*, 3.

Thus, it is not simply enough to mention that Islam is more than a legal tradition and then exclude the 'more' from one's analysis. If the basic Islamic worldview isn't taken into consideration, then Islamic law is judged within an alien paradigm, and, therefore, it is ipso facto nonsensical. This puts many Muslims in an impossible position where they find themselves trying to justify laws rooted in completely different underlying assumptions. This often results in apologetic, alienating, and unproductive dialogue. Sherman Jackson points out the mental struggle that Muslims go through in many liberal societies:

> And here we come to "the Muslim predicament," especially in the West. Because liberals have largely succeeded in monopolizing the meaning of the fundamental principles through which we negotiate modern life (freedom, equality, tolerance, rationality, etc.), Muslims find themselves only able to claim these when their claims comport with liberal definitions thereof. And when their scriptural sources or traditional authorities appear to be out of sync with these definitions, Muslims find themselves in the position of George Orwell's Winston: "How many fingers am I holding up, Winston?" From here they proceed, often on painfully tortuous logic, to try to reconcile every aspect of Islam with the reigning liberal paradigm. In this context, Muslims — and especially Muslim children — can never simply be themselves.[3]

Moreover, in an increasingly globalized world, this predicament is also felt by Muslims living in Muslim-majority nation-states. Nasr points out that "In many parts of the Islamic world, particularly in those countries where modern education is more prevalent, the younger generation has no knowledge of the intellectual and spiritual aspects of Islam and is completely defenseless against the onslaught of modernism."[4] The traditional Islamic penal code and its use of corporeal punishment provides a concrete example of the problem of cross-contextual understanding. According to the Quran, the punishment for theft is to cut off the hands of the thief:

> As for the thief, man or woman, cut off their hands as a requital for what they have earned. [That is] an exemplary punishment from Allah, and Allah is all-mighty, all-wise. (5:38)

---

[3] Sherman Jackson, "Liberalism and the American Muslim Predicament," *The Islamic Monthly*, June 27, 2015, https://www.theislamicmonthly.com/liberalism-and-the-american-muslim-predicament/.

[4] Nasr, *Ideals and Realities*, xxii.

When Muslims are questioned about their belief in this 'barbaric' practice, many of them become apologetic, defensive, and/or cognitively dissonant. This is understandable since this type of punishment can never be justified in a secular-liberal worldview wherein the individual and their body is considered autonomous and sacred. Hunt's work describes the different practices in the seventeenth and eighteenth centuries that worked towards changing the public conception of the body and the meaning of cruel and degrading punishment. This included "changes in musical and theatrical performances, domestic architecture and portraiture..."[5] Thus, Hunt writes that

> Once Enlightenment writers and legal reformers began to question torture and cruel punishment, an almost compete turnabout...took place... What was need in addition to empathy...was a new concern for the human body. Once sacred in only a religiously defined ordered...the body became sacred on its own in a secular order that rested in the autonomy and inviolability of humans.[6]

However, in terms of the general Islamic worldview, the punishment of cutting off the hands of the thief *can* be justified based on three principles: (1) the primacy of revelation, (2) pain as purification, and (3) the body as God's property. Before proceeding however, it is important to emphasize that I am not arguing for or against the reformation of the Islamic penal code and its use of corporeal punishment. Rather, I am arguing for the importance of understanding worldviews, that is, the ways in which people understand the world, and the influence this understanding has on a society's institutions and norms.[7] With this in mind, the first principle is the primacy of revelation. For Muslims, revelation is a form of Divine knowledge; therefore, it is the Quran – and not (liberal) reason – that should guide and govern the public sphere.[8] This is most clearly expressed in the verses that invoke the concept of the 'the

---

[5] Hunt, *Inventing Human Rights*, 83.
[6] Hunt, *Inventing Human Rights*, 81-82.
[7] It should be noted that these three principles can be expressed differently in different contexts. Therefore, to reiterate, my point is that Islamic law cannot be understood or reformed without first considering the Islamic worldview and its underlying principles.
[8] This doesn't mean that the Islamic law was always strictly applied in premodern Islamic societies; rather, it means that the Islamic worldview – in all of its expressions – largely determined or guided Muslim thought, norms, and laws. Even if Muslims initially accepted corporeal punishments because they were an established norm in seventh century Arabia, the argument still stands: one's sense of right and wrong is largely determined by their particular society and its underlying worldview.

limits of God' (*ḥudūd Allah*). These laws are generally considered God's rights over His creatures and are non-negotiable.[9] For example, the Qur'an reads:

> These are Allah's bounds, and whoever obeys Allah and His Apostle, He shall admit him to gardens with streams running in them, to remain in them [forever]. That is the great success. But whoever disobeys Allah and His Apostle and transgresses the bounds set by Allah, He shall make him enter a Fire, to remain in it [forever], and there will be a humiliating punishment for him. (04:13-14)

> You are permitted on the night of the fast to go into your wives: they are a garment for you, and you are a garment for them. Allah knew that you would betray yourselves, so He pardoned you and excused you. So now consort with them and seek what Allah has ordained for you, and eat and drink until the white streak becomes manifest to you from the dark streak at the crack of dawn. Then complete the fast until nightfall, and do not consort with them while you dwell in confinement in the mosques. These are Allah's bounds, so do not approach them. Thus does Allah clarify His signs for mankind so that they may be Godwary. (2:187)

> [Revocable] divorce may be only twice; then [let there be] either an honourable retention, or a kindly release. It is not lawful for you to take back anything from what you have given them, unless the couple fear that they may not maintain Allah's bounds; so if you fear they would not maintain Allah's bounds, there is no sin upon them in what she may give to secure her own release. These are Allah's bounds, so do not transgress them, and whoever transgresses the bounds of Allah—it is they who are the wrongdoers. (2:229)

Again, the point is that Muslims generally consider revelation – despite its varied interpretations – to be *the* source of all knowledge; therefore, they consider it to be a sacred repository containing guidance and governance for their individual and collective lives. Thus, the 'primacy of revelation' is the first of the three principles that allowed premodern Muslims to understand the 'cutting of hands' as a divinely ordained punishment, and not a 'barbaric'

---

[9] Kamali, *Shari'ah Law*, 22.

practice.[10] The second principle is that pain, in almost any form, including corporeal punishment, is a mode of spiritual purification.[11,12] According to the Islamic intellectual tradition, life is a test that aims to 'cleanse' human beings so that they can return to their 'pure' origin. On the subject of purification, Rafik Berjak notes, "Self-purity is...a major subject in Islam. The Prophet has said: 'Allah is pure and He shall not accept anything but purity'"[13] Thus, in this regard, the Quran states the following:

> ...Say, 'Even if you had remained in your houses, those destined to be slain would have set out toward the places where they were laid to rest, so that Allah may test what is in your breasts, and that He may purge what is in your hearts, and Allah knows well what is in the breasts.' (3:154)

> We will surely test you with a measure of fear and hunger and a loss of wealth, lives, and fruits; and give good news to the patient. (2:155)

According to *The Study Quran*, "Several *aḥadīth* indicate that the Prophet assured repentant thieves that had undergone the *ḥadd* punishment that they were forgiven by God and had been purified of their sin as a result of their punishment."[14] In the same light, there are also many hadith that explain pain as purification without reference to punishment. For example, it is reported that the Prophet said the following:

---

[10] The Qur'an invokes the 'limits/bounds of God' regularly. However, in relation to legal punishments, these 'limits' are contained to the six crimes of theft, adultery, false accusation of adultery, highway robbery, consumption of alcohol, and apostasy. The last two are problematic insofar as the Quran itself doesn't not prescribe any sort of worldly punishment for them.

[11] Pain can be understood as 'negative' purification because it is passive and comes directly or indirectly from God. On the other hand, 'positive' purification can be understood as active and involving religious practices such as praying and fasting.

[12] This does not include any self-inflicted physical pain. The latter is generally alien to the intellectual tradition's understanding of purification.

[13] Rafik Berajak, "'Purify," in *The Quran: An Encyclopedia*, ed. Oliver Leaman (New York: Routledge, 2006), 514.

[14] Nasr et al., *The Study Quran*, 296.

No fatigue, nor disease, nor sorrow, nor sadness, nor hurt, nor distress befalls a Muslim, even if it were the prick he receives from a thorn, but that Allah expiates some of his sins for that"[15]

It is also reported that the Prophet said that, "A believer's suffering removes his sins just as a blacksmith's fire removes slag from iron."[16] Thus, 'pain as purification' is the second of the three principles that allowed Muslims in premodern Islamic societies to understand the 'cutting of hands' as a punishment with a higher purpose and not a 'backwards' practice. The third principle is that the body – in a very real sense – belongs to God. According to the Quran, on the Day of Judgment the body will 'abandon' the human being and testify against the latter in service to God. The verse reads:

> …when they come to it, their hearing, their eyes and their skins will bear witness against them concerning what they used to do. They will say to their skins, 'Why did you bear witness against us?' They will say, 'We were given speech by Allah, who gave speech to all things. He created you the first time, and you are being brought back to Him. You did not use to conceal yourselves [while perpetrating sinful acts] lest your hearing, your eyes, or your skins should bear witness against you, but you thought that Allah did not know most of what you did. (41:20-22)

Thus, the idea that 'individuals have the right to do what they please with their own bodies' is alien to the Islamic worldview. Muslims generally understand that God has given people bodies so that they can use them to achieve success in this world and the hereafter. In this light, if a person uses the body to defy Divine laws and norms, then it is within God's right to do what He wills with that body. In any case, it is clear that the 'primacy of revelation', 'pain as purification', and the 'body belonging to God', combine to create a worldview wherein corporeal punishments, such as 'cutting the hands', have a higher purpose and 'make sense'. Thus, it is clear that worldviews have serious implications for human rights. Therefore, it is the deeper metaphysical, ontological, and epistemological principles that inform the Islamic worldview in general, and Islamic law in particular, that need to be addressed in any discussion concerning Islamic law, modernity, and human rights. Again, this is one of the reasons why I use the framework of Islamic traditionalism; it approaches

---

[15] Al-Bukhari, Book 75, Hadith 2, Sunnah: Sayings and Teachings of Prophet Muhammad, accessed April 1, 2017, https://sunnah.com/bukhari
[16] Tahera Qutbuddin, ed. and trans., *Light in the Heavens: Sayings of the Prophet Muhammad* (New York: New York University Press, 2016). Kindle.

traditional Islamic thought holistically and addresses the foundational questions that need to be answered in order to create any Islamic human rights model. Undoubtedly, the rights of a human being depend on their understanding of 'human', 'right', and 'the good'. It is only on this level that constructive dialogue can take place, and it is only on this level that effective and organic reform can happen. This point is also highlighted by Sachiko's work on gender in Islam when she correctly writes that

> The ultimate problem, when we speak of cross-cultural differences in the question of relationships among men and women, is that in a very real sense we have been living in different worlds. The cultural presuppositions of Westerners about what is important in life are profoundly different from the traditional views of Muslims or Japanese... I offer no answers as to whether or not Muslim women are any more oppressed than women elsewhere. *What I do maintain, however, is that generally the role of women in traditional Islam - not in any given Islamic society today - is consistent with the Islamic worldview.*[17]

Before proceeding to the following section on ethics and virtue, it is important to reiterate and clarify what I mean by the term 'Islamic intellectual tradition'. In general, this term refers to 1400-years of Islamic theology, philosophy, and mysticism. It includes the great and influential works of figures such as Al-Ghazâlî, ibn 'Arabī, and Mulla Sadra. More specifically and in relation to this book, however, I use the term 'Islamic intellectual tradition' to refer to Muslim traditionalists' specific understanding and explanation of Islam and premodern Islamic thought. Members of this school include figures such as Martin Lings, S. H. Nasr, and William Chittick. According to these Muslim traditionalists, the Islamic intellectual tradition, despite all of its differences, is a single tradition because it is rooted in the Quran and the latter's perennial truths. Moreover, in order to show that this particular perspective is indeed rooted in premodern Islamic thought, I also draw on two primary sources: the Quran and the thought of Imam Ali. As I have mentioned, one of my working assumptions is that this understanding of Islam represents an important and substantial 'Muslim voice' on the issue of Islam and modernity. This 'traditional voice' is expressed in many ways; nevertheless, in my opinion, it is unified in its basic intellectual and ethical orientation.

---

[17] Sachiko Murata, *The Tao of Islam: A Sourcebook on Gender Relationships in Islamic Thought* (Albany: State University of New York Press, 1992), 1. (Emphasis added)

The next section begins by looking at the Quran and its approach to morality. In doing so, it argues that the Quran supports the view that morality is intimately connected to spiritual transformation and virtue. Therefore, the section goes on to develop a theory of virtue ethics by addressing three main issues: the nature of reality; the nature of the human being and the Divine-human relationship; and the cultivation of virtue. The answers given to these issues constructs a theory of virtue ethics that is in line with the Islamic worldview and, therefore, has the ability to ground a model of human rights that is organic to the Islamic tradition as a whole. To reiterate, I believe that this approach is beneficial despite the fact that contemporary Muslim-majority states are no longer traditional in nature. This is because Muslims are more likely to accept 'reform' that is based on their own intellectual and cultural heritage.[18]

5.1. A Quranic perspective on morality and virtue

Since the twentieth century, consequentialism, deontology, and virtue ethics have dominated the field of moral philosophy. Consequentialism is based on the concept that 'what is right' is determined by the consequence of our actions. It argues that deciding how to act should not be determined by a rule or set of rules that may or may not lead to positive or beneficial consequences. In chapter three, I critically examined the secular-liberal ethical tradition's concept of consequentialism in the form of utilitarianism. In some instances, the Quran is also consequentialist in that it beseeches believers to act in a way that promotes well-being and helps people and their societies to flourish. For example,

> They ask you concerning wine and gambling. Say, 'There is a great sin in both of them, and some profits for the people, but their sinfulness outweighs their profit.' And they ask you as to what they should spend. Say, 'All that is surplus.' Thus does Allah clarify His signs for you so that you may reflect.[19]

---

[18] Nevertheless, is important to reiterate that I am primarily concerned with (1) drawing out the friction and overlap between traditional Islamic thought and contemporary human rights, and (2) constructing a theory of virtue ethics that has the ability to 'ground' an Islamic vision of human rights. Therefore, despite appearances to the contrary, I am not directly concerned with facilitating any socio-political reform in Muslim-majority nation-states today.
[19] My translation.

Al-Qurṭubī's commentary on this verse mentions the benefits and drawbacks of drinking wine and gambling, and in line with consequentialism, he proceeds to explain why the two activities lead to more negative consequences than positive ones. Islamic law eventually banned all intoxicants in light of one of the 'purposes of the shariah' (*maqāṣid al-sharīʿa*), namely, to 'protect human intelligence'.[20]

Despite verses such as 2:219, however, the Quranic injunction to do good is not generally rooted in utilitarian calculations. This is because the Quran repeatedly informs its readers that the value of action is wedded to faith. This is clearly expressed, for example, by the numerous verses that describe the righteous as people who believe *and* do good works:

> And give good news to those who have faith and do righteous deeds, that for them shall be gardens with streams running in them… (2:25)

> Indeed the faithful, the Jews, the Christians and the Sabaeans—those of them who have faith in Allah and the Last Day and act righteously—they shall have their reward from their Lord, and they will have no fear, nor will they grieve. (2:62)

> But as for those who have faith and do righteous deeds, He will pay them in full their rewards, and Allah does not like the wrongdoers. (3:57)

The idea that the value of action is interconnected with faith is also seen in the Quranic verses that describe the deeds of 'unbelievers'.[21] These verses imply that good action coupled with faithlessness is, at least in the final determination, wasted and futile:

> A parable of those who defy their Lord: their deeds are like ashes over which the wind blows hard on a tempestuous day: they have no power over anything they have earned. That is extreme error. (14:18)

> As for the faithless, their works are like a mirage in a plain, which the thirsty man supposes to be water. When he comes to it, he finds it to be

---

[20] Nasr et al., *The Study Quran*, 95.
[21] The term '*kafir*', which is commonly translated as 'unbeliever', does not have an equivalent in English. The term *kafir* more accurately denotes someone who knows the truth but rejects it anyway.

> nothing; but there he finds Allah, who will pay him his full account, and Allah is swift at reckoning. (24:39)

> ... So when there is panic, you see them looking at you, with their eyes rolling like someone fainting at death. Then, when the panic is over, they scald you with [their] sharp tongues in their greed for the spoils. They never have had faith. So Allah has made their works fail, and that is easy for Allah. (33:19)

Thus, the Quranic understanding of morality is not based on any form of consequentialism. A person can act, but, ultimately, it is the intention behind the act that is of utmost importance. The Quranic story of Prophet Abraham provides a further example of this principle. It describes Abraham as a young boy who snuck into the Kaaba in order to break the idols that were housed there. As a punishment, the people of Canaan decided to burn Abraham; however, according to the Quran, the young boy was saved when God issued a command to the fire and said: "We said, 'O fire! Be cool and safe for Abraham!'..."[22] Thus, the evil intention of the people subverted the effects of their actions. Of course, the subject of God and his relationship to the world has been debated in the Muslim world for centuries. Some maintain that verses such as 21:69 are metaphorical or symbolic, while others maintain they are literal and miraculous. Exploring this debate is beyond the scope of this work; however, it is sufficient to note that Muslims believe that – in one way or another – "God has power over all things." According to the Islamic intellectual tradition, faith and action are hierarchical but also self-reflexive. This is because faith or 'being' results in good action, and good action, in turn, strengthens faith. Thus, on the highest level, faith encompasses action and the two cannot be separated. For example, it is reported that Imam Ali heard the Prophet say that,

> Whoever says "there is no god except Allah" with sincere belief will enter the garden, his sincerity being that "no god except Allah" safeguards him from what Allah has forbidden.[23]

In a similar light, the Imam himself is reported to have said:

---

[22] 21:69-70
[23] Shaykh Fadhlalla Haeri, *Prophetic Traditions in Islam: On the Authority of the Family of the Prophet*, trans. Asadullah adh-Dhakir Yate (Zahra Publications, 2016). Kindle.

Faith...is recognition in the heart, and confirmation with the tongue, and action based on all the capabilities.[24]

In *Understanding Islam*, Schuon writes that, in Islam, the human being is primarily considered in terms of their intelligence and secondarily in terms of their will; therefore, it is the content of their intelligence *and then* the consequences of that content which ultimately 'saves' them.[25] However, this relationship between the Intellect and the will was inverted with the rise of the modern world. Nasr critiques Renaissance humanism and states that

> According to traditional doctrines our actions depend upon our mode of being [that is, faith] or, as the scholastics put it, *operari sequitur esse*. Pico, reversed this relationship and claimed that the "being of man follows from his doing." He thus stated...the primacy of action over contemplation and doing over being, which characterizes modern man and which has been of the greatest consequence for the destruction of the world of nature"[26]

Thus, according to the Quran and the Islamic intellectual tradition, considering the consequences of actions is important; however, in the ultimate determination, the consequences of actions are only truly good when they are a byproduct of sincere faith.

The second theory of morality, that is, deontology, is based on the concept that it is one's duty to act rightly, and 'what is right' is normally determined by a rule or set of rules. As I have argued, it is an incomplete form of deontology – that is, natural rights – that underpins the Universal Declaration of Human Rights. The Quran takes this deontological position to the extent that it gives human beings laws to follow in order to attain salvation. Thus, in this case, deontology is a form of Divine command theory because it is God and His will that determines the criterion for right and wrong action. This is illustrated by the following Quranic verses:

> These are Allah's bounds, and whoever obeys Allah and His Apostle, He shall admit him to gardens with streams running in them, to remain in

---

[24] Shaykh Fadhlalla Haeri, *The Sayings and Wisdom of Imam 'Ali* (Zahra Publications, 2018). Kindle.
[25] Frithjof Schuon, *Understanding Islam: A New Translation with Selected Letters*, ed. Patrick Laude (Bloomington: World Wisdom, 2011), 2.
[26] Chittick, ed., *Essential Seyyed Hossein Nasr*, 144-5.

them [forever]. That is the great success. But whoever disobeys Allah and His Apostle and transgresses the bounds set by Allah, He shall make him enter a Fire, to remain in it [forever], and there will be a humiliating punishment for him. (04:13-14)

Warfare has been prescribed for you, though it is repulsive to you. Yet it may be that you dislike something, which is good for you, and it may be that you love something, which is bad for you, and Allah knows and you do not know. (2:216)

The Apostle and the faithful have faith in what has been sent down to him from his Lord. Each [of them] has faith in Allah, His angels, His scriptures and His apostles. They declare, 'We make no distinction between any of His apostles.' And they say, 'We hear and obey. Our Lord, forgive us, and toward You is the return.' (2:285)

Thus, these verses seem to point to the fact that an action is good because God wills it and not vice versa. However, the Islamic intellectual tradition was somewhat divided on this issue, and the question – what makes an action good? – prompted one of the earliest debates in Islamic history.[27] Nevertheless, after the death of the Prophet, deontology, in the form of Divine command theory, virtually dominated the field of Islamic ethics. This is particularly true when it came to the Islamic legal tradition and the jurists who presided over it. This is because Islamic societies, at least in principle, are nomocracies. In this regard, Majjid Khadduri writes the following:

> In a society which presupposes that man is essential weak and therefore incapable of rising above personal failings…a superhuman or Divine authority is invoked to provide either the sources or the basic principles of the public order under which a certain standard of justice is established… The justice which flows from such a high Divine source is considered applicable to all men and forms another category of justice. In contrast with positive justice, it may be called Divine or revelational justice… It is therefore the Law, embodying the principles of Divine authority, which indeed rules and wherefore the state

---

[27] Steffen Stelzer, "Ethics," in *The Cambridge Companion to Classical Islamic Theology*, ed. Tim Winter (Cambridge: Cambridge University Press, 2008), 161-79.

becomes not, strictly speaking, a theocracy, but…might be called a Divine nomocracy.[28]

The centrality of Islamic law expressed in the form of 'God's will', was also the result of a number of contextual factors; arguably, the most important of these was the rapid growth of the Islamic empire and the concomitant need to provide order for the growing population. Despite this focus on Divine command theory, however, there are many verses in the Quran that seem to oppose the view that ethics is *exclusively* restricted to acting in accordance with God's will as expressed in the Quran. As the following verses indicate, the Quran is also concerned with something above and beyond outward obedience to the Divine law:

> The Bedouins say, 'We have faith.' Say, 'You do not have faith yet; rather, say, "We have embraced Islam," for faith has not yet entered into your hearts. Yet if you obey Allah and His Apostle, He will not stint anything of [the reward of] your works. Indeed Allah is all-forgiving, all-merciful.' (49:14)

> Call them after their fathers. That is more just with Allah. If you do not know their fathers, then they are your brethren in the faith and your kinsmen. Excepting what your hearts may intend deliberately, there will be no sin upon you for any mistake that you may make therein. And Allah is all-forgiving, all-merciful. (33:5)

> the day when neither wealth nor children will avail, except him who comes to Allah with a sound heart. (26:88-89)

According to Ibn Kathīr's commentary on verse 49:14, "belief is of a higher rank than submission," and that the desert Arabs "had simply not yet attained faith" through submission.[29] Similarly, according to al-Qurṭubi's commentary on verse 26:29, a "sound heart" refers to the heart's knowledge that "God is real, that the Hereafter will come, and that God will resurrect what is in the Graves."[30] Other commentators take the concept of a sound heart further, and maintain that it refers to spiritual healthiness, a heart emptied of the world and filled with the

---

[28] Khadduri, *Islamic Conception*, 3-4. Khadduri contrasts this view with what he calls 'positive justice', that is, justice based on the assumption that people are capable of determining their own interests and needs based on their experience and reasoning.
[29] Nasr et al., *The Study Quran*, 1262.
[30] Nasr et al., *The Study Quran*, 915.

love of God.³¹ Thus, according to these verses, it can be argued that the Quran places more importance on 'being' than on 'doing'. As such, the Quran seems to imply that the most important aspect of good actions is that they are transformative. That is, they transform human into virtuous beings who use their Intellect/Heart in conjunction with any outward expression of God's will. The Islamic intellectual tradition picked up on this view of ethics as intimately connected to one's spiritual state, and not simply outward action. For example, in *The Peak*, Imam Ali states the following:

> The doer of good is better than the good itself, and the doer of evil is worse than the evil itself.³²

> The sin that displeases you is better in the view of Allah than the virtue that makes you proud.³³

> Understand information you hear with the reasoning of responsibility not the reasoning of the reporter,
> for there are many reports of knowledge but few are responsible.³⁴

Thus, one can see the primary importance that the Quran and the Islamic intellectual tradition place on the state of a person's being. Therefore, from this point of view, it is clear that any Islamic theory of ethics and human rights must be grounded in the concept of spiritual transformation leading to virtuous character. Thus, virtue theory moves away from attempting to determine the right course of action in any given situation; rather, it situates ethics within a broader framework concerning the purpose of human existence. It maintains that the actions of a 'good person' are good actions and the actions of a 'bad person' are bad. In other words, right action is derived from virtue and not vice versa.³⁵ Thus, virtue theory addresses the fundamental issues concerning human existence and 'being' that need to be answered in order to construct any theory of human rights. These are: the

---

[31] Nasr et al., *The Study Quran*, 915.
[32] *The Peak*, saying number 32.
[33] *The Peak*, saying number 46.
[34] As quoted in Thomas Cleary, *Living and Dying with Grace: Counsels of Hadrat Ali* (Boston: Shambhala Publications, 1996), 14. In other words, the Imam is saying that knowledge is about understanding and transformation as opposed to memorization and regurgitation.
[35] Virtue is primary in principle. However, virtue and virtuous action are also self-reflexive because they function to develop and reinforce each other.

nature of reality; the nature of the human being and the Divine-human relationship; and the cultivation of virtue. In the Islamic context then, I argue that a human rights society is one that is organized in a way that allows people to achieve their primary purpose in life. As I argue in the next section, this is a virtuous character in this world leading to felicity in the hereafter.

In concluding this section of the chapter, it is important to reiterate two points. The first is that human rights are informed by a particular society's understanding about the meaning and purpose of life. Thus, it is only on this 'underlying level of thought' that genuine discourse and reform can take place – including reform in the area of Islamic law. As Sa'diyya Shaikh points out in her attempt to negotiate gender understandings:

> Traditional Muslim personal law is constrained by its own underlying notion of human nature. From a contemporary Islamic feminist perspective, the limited gender understandings of human nature, as developed in different sociohistorical contexts, serves as central deficits in various iterations of classical Islamic law. The problematic may be called a short-coming in gendered 'religious anthropology', a term that addresses questions of what it means to be a human being from a religious perspective… In the Muslim tradition, Sufi thinkers in particular have provided detailed discussions on the human condition… and the ways in which the fundamental theological imperative of submission provides the ontological basis for the juridic-ethical legacy and related norms of sociability[36]

The second point is that contemporary Islamic thought's primary goal is to establish a standard of judgment that can be applied to the religion's sacred texts in order to separate the universal from the relative. This, in turn, creates a space for reform in light of the changing circumstances of any given society. The following section constructs such a standard; namely, a virtue theory based on Muslim traditionalist's articulation of the Islamic worldview and its specific understanding of reality, the human being, and virtue. In my opinion, any method that dismisses or reduces these essential ideas of Islamic thought

---

[36] Sa'diyya Shaikh, "Islamic Law, Sufism and Gender: Rethinking the Terms of the Debate," in *Men in Charge? Rethinking Authority in Muslim Legal Tradition*, ed. Ziba Mir-Hosseini, Mulki Al-Sharmani and Jana Rumminger (London: Oneworld Pub., 2015), 106-7. I don't agree that Islamic 'religious anthropology' is limited, deficient, or necessarily problematic on a whole. However, I do agree that 'religious anthropology' is the foundation of Islamic law and needs to be explored in any fruitful discussion of Islamic ethics and its relationship to modernity and human rights.

is bound to fail insofar as its approach and conclusions will be alien to the Islamic tradition as a whole and the 'Muslim mentality' that it represents.

5.2. Traditional Islamic virtue theory

Muslims understand Islam as the final expression of the primordial religion intended for humanity. Its primordiality is attested to by Quranic passages that apply the word 'Muslim' to people who came before the Prophet's time. In this case, the word 'Muslim' can be understood as a verbal noun that refers to the act of submitting to God. For example, the Quran reads:

> When Jesus sensed their faithlessness, he said, 'Who will be my helpers on the path toward Allah?' The Disciples said, 'We will be helpers of Allah. We have faith in Allah, and you be witness that we are Muslims [that is, submitters to His will]. (3:52)[37]

> And wage jihad for the sake of Allah, a jihad which is worthy of Him. He has chosen you and has not placed for you any obstacle in the religion, the faith of your father, Abraham. He named you 'Muslims' before, and in this, so that the Apostle may be a witness to you, and that you may be witnesses to mankind…. (22:78)

On the other hand, Islam's finality is based on the Quranic verses that refers to the Prophet as the seal of the Prophets (*khātam an-nabīyīn*). The Quran tells the believers that

> Muhammad is not the father of any man among you, but he is the Apostle of Allah and the Seal of the Prophets, and Allah has knowledge of all things. (33:40)

These verses are further strengthened by the hadith literature. For example, in a well-known saying, the Prophet describes himself as the final brick completing the building of a beautiful house.[38] Thus, according to Muslims, guidance from God in the form of prophecy and revelation ended with the Prophet. In this light, Nasr describes three ways in which Islam can be understood:

> In its universal sense, Islam may be said to have three levels of meaning. All beings in the universe, to begin with, are Muslim, i.e.,

---

[37] Translation mine.
[38] Al-Bukhari, book 43, hadith 23.

"surrendered to the Divine Will." (A flower cannot help being a flower; a diamond cannot do other than sparkle. God has made them so; it is theirs to obey.) Secondly, all men who accept with their will the sacred law of the revelation are Muslim in that they surrender their will to that law...Finally, we have the level of pure knowledge and understanding. It is that of the contemplative, the gnostic ('arif), the level that has been recognized throughout Islamic history as the highest and most comprehensive. The gnostic is Muslim in that his whole being is surrendered to God; he has no separate individual existence of his own. He is like the birds and the flowers in his yielding to the Creator; like them, like all the other elements of the cosmos, he reflects the Divine Intellect to his own degree. He reflects it actively, however, they passively; his participation is a conscious one.[39]

In any case, Islam – like the religions that preceded it – provides its followers with both a doctrine of reality and a method of transformation to that reality. This brings me to the first question and the basis of this book's theory of virtue ethics: what is the Islamic intellectual tradition's doctrine of reality?

The Quran's central doctrine is the existence and oneness of God (*tawhid*). In this regard, the Quran states:

Say, 'He is Allah, the One. Allah is the All-embracing. He neither begat, nor was begotten, nor has He any equal.' (112:1-4)

That is because Allah is the Reality, and whatever they invoke besides Him is nullity, and because Allah is the All-exalted, the All-great. (31:30)

According to Ṭabāṭabā'ī's commentary on 31:30:

This verse is thus understood as an affirmation that God is the Ultimate Reality beyond and behind all of creation and that all of the things to which anyone ascribes ultimate power...are entirely dependent upon God, possessing no reality in and of themselves. God is the only reality or being that is necessary, while all other things are contingent.[40]

---

[39] Seyyed Hossein Nasr, *Science and Civilization in Islam* (Illinois: ABC International Group, 2001), 23.
[40] Nasr et al., *The Study Quran*, 1007.

This view that God is Reality itself is further supported by the Imam, and his answer to a question concerning the nature of God:

> He is Allah, the Clear Truth, truer and clearer than the eyes perceive. The intellects cannot reach Him by any definition...and the imagination cannot reach Him by any evaluation. There is no beginning to His primacy and there is no end to His eternity. He is the First and the Eternal, and He is the Everlasting without end... He gave all things limitations when He created them, so as to make it clear that He is not like them[41]

The concept of *tawhid* is one of the underlying principles that functioned to unify Muslims and Islamic societies across different spacio-temporal boundaries. In fact, an astounding degree of Islamic thought and culture is an expression of the principle of *tawhid*. For example, in terms of Islamic intellectuality, Chittick notes that

> The intellectual tradition was robust and lively, so disagreements...were common. Nonetheless, in all the different schools of thought that have appeared over Islamic history...one principle has always been agreed upon: God is one, and he is the only source of Truth and Reality: He is the origin of all things, and all things return to him.[42]

How exactly does the Quranic idea of *tawhid* explain the nature of reality? Muslim traditionalists explain *tawhid* by pointing to the fact that God is both absolute and infinite. The quality of God's absoluteness means that He is complete unity or oneness. The quality of God's infinitude means that God contains all possibilities within Himself and that these possibilities are realized through the process of creation.[43] Therefore, the Islamic traditionalism's doctrine of reality is that nothing is truly real except the ultimate Reality, that is, God. For example, Chittick writes that "Islamic forms of thinking take it for granted that God is the source of all reality. The universe and all things within it appear from God in stages, just as light appears from the sun in degrees."[44] Coomaraswamy also draws on the symbolism of the sun and writes that "from the spiritual perspective what we call the world-process and creation is ... a

---

[41] Haeri, *Sayings and Wisdom*.
[42] William C. Chittick, *Science of the Cosmos, Science of the Soul: The Pertinence of Islamic Cosmology in the Modern World* (Oxford: Oneworld Publication, 2007), 7.
[43] Nasr, *Heart of Islam*, 9-10.
[44] Chittick, *Science of the Cosmos*, 42

game that the Spirit plays with itself, as sunlight 'plays' upon whatever it illuminates and quickens, although unaffected by its apparent contacts."[45] This means that, from a metaphysical perspective, Muslim traditionalists explain *tawhid* as the oneness of Reality and its corollary: the illusionary, temporary, and derivative nature of all creation.[46] The Quran states:

> Everyone on it is ephemeral, yet lasting is the majestic and munificent Face of your Lord. (55:26-27)

Imam Ali also echoes the same understanding of the created world with the following advice:

> Be informed that this world which you have started to covet, and in which you are interested, and which sometimes enrages you and sometimes pleases you, is not your (permanent) abode, nor is it the place of your stay for which you might have been created, nor is it the one to which you have been invited. Be informed that it will not last for you, nor will you live along with it…[47]

Based on this understanding of *tawhid*, it can be said that all creation is an ontological movement away from God. This, in turn, means that there are degrees of reality and a creature is 'real' to the extent that it 'climbs back up creation' by conforming to God. As I go on to argue, 'conforming to God' is the goal of human existence and, therefore, needs to ground any Islamic theory of human rights. However, before discussing this goal and its connection to virtue, it is important to first look at the Islamic intellectual tradition's understanding of human nature and the Divine-human relationship. This is because these two concepts, along with *tawhid*, form the foundation of this book's virtue ethics.

The Quran describes the human condition in terms of polarity. On the one hand, humans are among the noblest of creatures that dwell on earth with the 'Spirit of God' within them:

> When your Lord said to the angels, 'Indeed I am about to create a human being out of clay. So when I have proportioned him and

---

[45] As quoted in Perry N. Whitall, ed., *A Treasury of Traditional Wisdom: An Encyclopedia of Humankind's Spiritual Truth*, 3rd ed. (Louisville: Fons Vitae, 2000), 23.
[46] The 'oneness of reality' is not a widely accepted belief; however, this is not problematic since virtually all Muslims believe that God is the single source of all reality.
[47] *The Peak*, Sermon 172.

> breathed into him of My spirit, then fall down in prostration before him.' (38:71-72)

> Certainly We have honoured the Children of Adam, and carried them over land and sea, and provided them with all the good things, and preferred them with a complete preference over many of those We have created. (17:70)

On the other hand, however, The Quran also describes human as created from dust and inclined towards ingratitude, heedlessness, and ignorance:

> Of His signs is that He created you from dust, then, behold, you are humans scattering [all over]! (30:20)

> [This is] a promise of Allah: Allah does not break His promise, but most people do not know. They know just an outward aspect of the life of the world, but they are oblivious of the Hereafter. (30:6-7)

> It is He who made for you hearing, eyesight, and hearts. Little do you thank. It is He who created you on the earth, and you will be mustered toward Him. And it is He who gives life and brings death, and due to Him is the alternation of day and night. Do you not exercise your reason? (23:78-80)

Oliver Leaman rightly argues that the concept of redemption has its basis in the Quran; therefore, it is not a 'Christian reading' of Islamic doctrines. In this regard, he writes that

> It is often said that Islam believes that humankind is basically good and so there is no need for God to redeem us... However, the angels suggest that if humans were given their head, they would succumb to corruption and shed bled (2.30) ...[Moreover,] The Quran notes that Satan tempts the 'Children of Adam' (7.26-27), and describes us as feeble (4.28), despairing (11.9), unjust (14.34), quarrelsome (16.4) tyrannical (96.6) and lost (105.2)...The rather pessimistic conclusion to all this is that 'Most men are not believers' (12.103) ... [and] 'If God were to punish humans for their wrongdoing, He would not leave a single creature'(16.61).[48]

---

[48] Oliver Leaman, "Sin," in *The Quran: An Encyclopedia*, ed. Oliver Leaman (New York: Routledge, 2006), 593.

In any case, this duality is captured by the Islamic intellectual tradition's understanding that humans have the potential to be better than angels or worse than animals. This is possible because God gave humans the gift of free will; therefore, they are the only creatures that can choose to obey or disobey God. Schuon's poetry refers to these two human poles:

> Most animals are horizontal, since
> Their homeland is not other than this Earth;
> But man's essential stance is vertical;
> Free will to choose Salvation proves his worth.[49]

The Imam's constant admonitions also generally presuppose that duality and free will are inherent to the human state. More specifically, a man asked Imam Ali if they had been destined to fight, and the Imam answered that, if by 'destiny' the man meant 'forced by compulsion', then it was not the case. This is because

> if it were so, there would have been no question of reward or chastisement and there would have been no sense in Allah's promises or warnings. (On the other hand) Allah, the Glorified One, has ordered His servants to act according to their free will and has cautioned them and protected them (from evil) [by advising them to what is best] ...[50]

In terms of the two human poles, the Quran continuously instructs, warns, and encourages humans to achieve their higher nature. Again, to *be* one's highest self by 'conforming to God' is the purpose of life. Hence, this doctrine and its consequences must be at the core of any Islamic concept of human rights. Again, this is discussed in the following section on the cultivation of virtue. First, however, it is important to understand the Islamic intellectual tradition's explanation of the Divine-human relationship, because it is this relationship that leads to this book's specific vision of virtue.

The Quran also speaks about the relationship between God and humans in two ways. First and foremost, the human being is the servant of God ('*abd Allah*). According to the Quran, God assembled the children of Adam and asked them: Am I not your Lord? They testified in the affirmative, and it is because of this testimony that human beings cannot plead ignorance on the Day of Judgment (*Yawm al-Qiyāmah*). Of course, many people would

---

[49] Frithjof Schuon, *Road to the Heart: Poems* (Bloomington: World Wisdom, 2003), 62.
[50] *The Peak*, Saying 78.

question this perspective and claim that they do not remember anything of the sort. In response, the Islamic intellectual tradition places particular emphasis on the connection between forgetfulness and evil, and it maintains that the Prophets, Scriptures, and other signs of God all operate to remind humans of what they already know.[51] For example, the Quran says,

> …almost exploding with rage. Whenever a group is thrown in it, its keepers will ask them, 'Did not any warner come to you?' They will say, 'Yes, a warner did come to us, but we belied him and said, 'Allah did not send down anything; you are only in great error.' And they will say, 'Had we listened or used our intellects, we would not have been among inmates of the Fire' (67:8-10)[52]

> Who is a greater wrongdoer than he who is reminded of the signs of his Lord, whereat he disregards them and forgets what his hands have sent ahead? Indeed We have cast veils on their hearts lest they should understand it, and a deafness into their ears; and if you invite them to guidance they will never [let themselves] be guided. (18:57)

This is why, throughout Islamic history, practicing Muslims have paid particular attention to perpetuating the remembrance of God. In this regard, the Imam tells his listeners:

> Increase your remembrance of Allah, for it is the best of remembrances, and desire what has been promised to those who live their lives fearing Him - for his Promise is the truest of promises…[53]

> Perpetuate the dhikr, for truly it illumines the heart and it is the most excellent form of worship.[54]

In any case, according to the Quranic narrative, humanity not only testified to the existence of God but also willingly accepted the 'station of servanthood'. The verse of 'the Trust' reads:

---

[51] Shah-Kazemi, *Justice and Remembrance*, 150-1.
[52] Translation mine.
[53] As quoted in Camille Helminski, ed., *The Book of Character: An Anthology of Writing on Virtue from Islamic and Other Sources* (Bristol: The Book Foundation, 2005), 9.
[54] Shah-Kazemi, *Justice and Remembrance*, 138.

> Indeed We presented the Trust to the heavens and the earth and the mountains, but they refused to undertake it and were apprehensive of it; but man undertook it. Indeed he is most unjust and ignorant. Allah will surely punish the hypocrites, men and women, and the polytheists, men and women, and Allah will turn clemently to the faithful, men and women, and Allah is all-forgiving, all-merciful. (33:72-73)

Although humans were 'unjust and ignorant', God provided them with the ability to fulfill their trust, and this leads us to the second relationship between God and humans; namely, that the latter are God's representatives on earth. The Quran explains this relationship through its narrative of Prophet Adam, who is considered to be the prototype for humanity. According to the Quran, God breathed His Spirit into Adam and taught him the 'name of things':

> When your Lord said to the angels, 'Indeed I am about to create a human being out of clay. So when I have proportioned him and breathed into him of My spirit, then fall down in prostration before him.' There at the angels prostrated, all of them together, but not Iblis; he acted arrogantly and he was one of the faithless. (38:71-74)

According to al-Ṭabarī, the term 'Spirit' refers to God's power. Others, such as al-Razi, maintain that this verse refers to the creation of the human soul, and that the latter, being 'of God', is a heavenly, noble, and holy faculty.[55] In terms of the 'name of things', the Quran reads:

> And He taught Adam the Names, all of them; then presented them to the angels and said, 'Tell me the names of these, if you are truthful.' (31) They said, 'Immaculate are You! We have no knowledge except what You have taught us. Indeed You are the All-knowing, the All-wise.' (32) He said, 'O Adam, inform them of their names,' and when he had informed them of their names, He said, 'Did I not tell you that I know the Unseen of the heavens and the earth, and that I know whatever you disclose and whatever you conceal?' (2:31-33)

According to some Quranic commentators, such as ibn ʿArabī, the 'names of things' refers to the knowledge of all reality.[56] According to Chittick, 'the names' were taught to Adam within the context of God's knowledge; therefore,

---

[55] Nasr et al., *The Study Quran,* 1114.
[56] Nasr et al., *The Study Quran,* 22.

they denote the essence or inward reality of things in accordance with the function and role of human beings.[57] Of course, if humans were not able to have this knowledge of God, the cosmos, and the soul, as well as the power to act on this knowledge, then they would not have the ability to serve and represent God on earth. Nasr brings together this two-fold relationship between humans and God by explaining that

> Man was taught the name of all things as the Quran states: "And He taught Adam all the names," (II; 31), meaning that he was given power and dominion over all things by virtue of being God's vicegerent (*khalifah*) on earth. But with this function of *khalifah* was combined the quality of `abd, that is, the quality of being in perfect submission to God. Man has the right to dominate over the earth as *khalifah* only on the condition that he remains in perfect submission to Him who is the real master of nature. The mastery and power of man over nature is only a borrowed power given to man because he reflects the Divine Names and Qualities.[58]

The Quranic narrative of Adam goes on to say that Satan tempted Adam and Eve to eat from the 'forbidden tree'; in doing so, they were banished from heaven and sent down to earth:

> So they both ate of it, and their nakedness became evident to them, and they began to stitch over themselves with the leaves of paradise. Adam disobeyed his Lord, and went amiss. Then his Lord chose him, and turned to him clemently, and guided him. He said, 'Get down both of you from it, all together, being enemies of one another! Yet, should any guidance come to you from Me, those who follow My guidance will not go astray, nor will they be miserable. But whoever disregards My remembrance, his shall be a wretched life, and We shall raise him blind on the Day of Resurrection.' (20:121-124)

Ultimately, God forgave Adam and Eve, and He assured them that he would send help to their 'children' and guide whomever remembered Him. Thus, human beings have the responsibility to fulfill their trust by serving and

---

[57] Chittick, *Science of the Cosmos*, 84-5.
[58] S. H. Nasr, "Who is Man? The Perennial Answer of Islam," in *The Sword of Gnosis*, ed. Jacob Needleman (Baltimore: Penguin Books Inc., 1974), 207.

representing God on earth. Again, they have the power to do this because of their 'Divine Breath' and their knowledge of the 'names of things'.

Based on this perspective of the Divine-human relationship, it can be stated that the 'station of servanthood' is the basis for human responsibilities, and that the 'station of representation' is the basis for human rights. In other words, human responsibilities are based on the fact that human beings are servants of God and, therefore, they are responsible to Him for the way they live their lives. On the other hand, human rights are based on the fact that all human beings have the ability to represent God on earth and, therefore, they are all equal in their Divine potential. However, the 'station of servanthood' and concomitant idea of human responsibility is primary in the Islamic worldview and the general Muslim mentality. In this regard, Nasr writes the following:

> ...[The] one basic element with which all schools of Islamic though and in fact ordinary believers agree is the truth that God is our creator, or, philosophically speaking, the ontological cause of our existence. It is therefore we who owe everything to Him and our rights derive from our fulfilling our responsibilities towards Him and Obeying His will.[59]

As I go on to argue, it is the primacy of human responsibilities that is one of the main reasons for the friction between Islam and the secular-liberal tradition in general, and Islam and contemporary human rights in particular.

Thus far, my theory of virtue ethics points to the fact that God is the one and only reality and 'all else' has an illusionary, temporary, and/or derivative mode of existence. It also maintains that the goal of human beings is to use their free will to serve and represent God on Earth. The next section discusses this Divine-human relationship and its connection to cultivating virtue. It argues that human beings serve and represent God to the extent that they conform to Him through virtuous transformation. Again, these ideas must form the basis of any Islamic human rights theory because human rights are derived from a particular society's worldview, underlying assumptions, and understanding of the purpose of human existence.

As mentioned, human beings can only serve and represent God to the extent that they are able to conform themselves to God. This conformity denotes a person's state of 'being' rather than their 'doing'. In this regard, this section begins by exploring the Quran and Islamic intellectual tradition's understanding of the heart as the 'place' of knowing and being. Then, it goes

---

[59] Nasr, *Heart of Islam*, 277.

on to explore the idea of virtue as the realization of God's Names and Qualities in the human Heart. Finally, it concludes by discussing this understanding of virtue and its relation to ethics. Kazemi succinctly brings together the ideas in this section in his explanation of spiritual virtue. He writes that the latter "engages all that one is. One has to *be* good before one *does* good.; and the only way 'to be', is to be at one with the Real, which alone 'is'.[60]

In the modern world, the ability to know the truth is generally attributed to the mind and the human ability to reason and experience. This understanding gained prominence with the rise of modernity and its philosophies, such as Descartes' dualism and Spinoza's axioms. However, this epistemological model is alien to the Quran and the Islamic intellectual tradition as a whole. For Muslim traditionalists, human reason is important and necessary; however, it is considered to be a derivative and secondary mode of knowing. This is because human reason needs to be 'grounded' in the objective principles of revelation *and* virtue in order to operate properly. Without this, reason quickly descends into rationalization based on changing circumstances and sentiments. In any case, according to the Quran and the Islamic intellectual tradition, true and objective knowledge is a product of the human 'Heart'. According to the Quran:

> Have they not travelled through the land so that they may have hearts by which they may exercise their reason, or ears by which they may hear? Indeed, it is not the eyes that turn blind, but it is the hearts in the breasts that turn blind! (22:46)

> Indeed, it is [present as] manifest signs in the breasts of those who have been given knowledge, and none contests Our signs except wrongdoers. (29:49)

Imam Ali's words mirror the Quranic understanding of the 'knowing heart':

> Righteous struggle is of three types: the first thing to be overcome in this struggle is the hand, then the tongue, then the heart, Once the heart cannot recognize good or decry evil, it is upended and turned topsy-turvey.[61]

---

[60] Shah-Kazemi, *Justice and Remembrance*, 77.
[61] As quoted in Tahera Qutbuddin, ed. and trans., *A Treasury of Virtues and One Hundred Proverbs* (New York: New York University Press, 2013). Kindle.

The eyes cannot perceive Him with the sense of sight, but the heart can perceive Him through the realities of trust...[62]

Writing from this perspective, Ali Lakhani points out that

> ...Truth, being of a universal order, is inscribed within our deepest selves - that within us which is transcendent and universal, our primordial nature, the core of our very being.... The faculty which is capable of discerning reality in its more subtle nature...[is] the transcendent faculty of the supra-rational Intellect the core of our discerning self...[63]

According to the Quran and the Islamic intellectual tradition, the Heart is the place of knowledge *and* the place of 'being'. This is because the Heart is the meeting place between the Divine and human natures; therefore, it is the place where the knower and the known converge. In other words, knowledge and being are inseparable from one another and one cannot know God without '*realizing* God'. This idea is alluded to in two hadiths wherein God is speaking through the Prophet:

> My servant draws near to Me by nothing dearer to Me than that which I have established as a duty for him. And My servant does not cease to approach Me through supererogatory acts until I love him. And when I love him, I become his hearing with which he hears, his sight with which he sees, his hand with which he grasps, and his foot with which he walks. And if he asks Me [for something], I give it to him. If he seeks refuge with Me, I place him under My protection..."[64]

> Neither My earth nor My heaven hath room for Me, but the heart of my believing servants hath room for me.[65]

Chittick also connects the ideas of knowledge, realization, and virtue by writing the following:

---

[62] Haeri, *Sayings and Wisdom*.
[63] Ali M. Lakhani, "The Metaphysics of Human Governance: Imam 'Alī, Truth and Justice," in *The Sacred Foundations of Justice in Islam: The Teachings of 'Alī ibn Abī Ṭālib* (Bloomington: World Wisdom, 2006), 6.
[64] Ibn 'Arabī, *Divine Sayings: The Mishkāt al-Anwār of Ibn 'Arabi*, trans. Stephen Hirtenstein and Martin Nottcut (Anqa Publishing, 2004). Kindle. 70.
[65] Lings, *Ancient Beliefs*, 43

> One of the fruits of intellectual learning was to...see and realize...that the so- called "object" out there and "subject" in here are essentially the same. To think of the two as sperate is to falsify the meaning of cosmos and soul, to distort the relationship between things and self... The very structure of the intellectual quest stressed not only the achievement of right knowledge through unification of the subject and the object, but also the actualization of sound moral character and the cultivation of virtue.[66]

If the Heart is the place of knowledge and being, what exactly do humans have to know and realize in relation to God? The school of Islamic traditionalism is specifically concerned with knowing God as He revealed Himself in the Quran, that is, through His and His Divine Names and Qualities.[67] This includes titles such as the Truth, the Merciful, the Generous, and the Wise. According to this view, the Names and Qualities of God are not simply mental abstractions; they are ontological realities that can be known and realized by human beings. For example, *The Study Quran*'s commentary on verse 7:180, which encourages the faithful to call on God by His most beautiful Names, states that

> ...Each Name is understood to possess a real Divine Presence or Quality, for as al-Tabrisi notes there are no empty titles for God. In fact, in Islamic metaphysics, the whole of the cosmos is considered to be in reality nothing but reflection or theophanies...of the Divine Names and Qualities... [Moreover] in Islamic esoterism, God and His Names are considered one. God is understood to be present in His sanctified Names, each of which is a ladder leading to Him.[68]

These Names of God are the virtues.[69] Realizing these virtues allows human beings to return to their primordial, complete, and theomorphic selves (*al-insān al-kāmil*). It is in relation to this state that humans 'are' ethical and,

---

[66] Chittick, *Science of the* Cosmos, 136.

[67] One may object on the grounds that this is a Sufi point of view. However, this objection is misleading for two reasons. First, the so-called 'Sufis' were not an isolated group; rather, they were part and parcel of the larger Muslim community. Second, over the years, and through figures such as Al-Ghazâlî, much 'Sufi thought' was integrated into mainstream Islamic thought.

[68] Nasr et al., *The Study Quran*, 472.

[69] It is important to note that some Names of God, such as 'the Holy', are restricted to God alone.

consequently, act ethically. According to Kazemi's understanding of Imam Ali's ethical and spiritual ethos: "the 'true intellectual'…is one who not only *thinks* correctly but also *acts* ethically, and, at the deepest level, one who seeks to *realize* the ultimate Reality."[70] How does one arrive at this complete and virtuous human state?

As mentioned, the Quran and Islamic intellectual tradition emphasize the connection between forgetfulness and evil on the one hand, and remembrance and goodness on the other hand. For example, the Quran states

> … the men who remember Allah greatly and the women who remember… Allah holds in store for them forgiveness and a great reward. (33:35)

> Recite what has been revealed to you of the Book, and maintain the prayer. Indeed the prayer restrains from indecent and wrongful conduct, and the remembrance of Allah is surely greater. And Allah knows whatever [deeds] you do. (29:45)

> Content yourself with the company of those who supplicate their Lord morning and evening, desiring His Face, and do not lose sight of them, desiring the glitter of the life of this world. And do not obey him whose heart We have made oblivious to Our remembrance, and who follows his own desires, and whose conduct is [mere] profligacy. (18:28)

Imam Ali also underscores the importance of remembrance on the journey towards God:

> Whoever remembers Allah, glory be to Him, Allah enlivens his heart and illuminates his intellect and the innermost core of his heart.[71]

> Perpetuate the dhikr, for truly it illuminates the heart and is the most excellent form of worship.[72]

> Everyone who lacks self-restraint and piety will have a dead heart; whoever has a dead heart will enter inside the Hell.[73]

---

[70] Shah-Kazemi. *Justice and Remembrance*, 35.
[71] Muhammadi M. Rayshahri, ed., *The Scale of Wisdom: A Compendium of Shi'a Ḥadīth* (London: ICAS Press), 412.
[72] As quoted in Shah-Kazemi, *Justice and Remembrance*, 138.

Thus, the Heart needs to be 'reminded' about the reality of *tawhid* in the created order. From this perspective, 'realization through remembrance' is also the primary purpose for the revealed law, as well as the different Islamic rites and rituals. For example, Chittick summarizes ibn 'Arabī's explanation of realizing the virtues, that is, God's Divine Names and Qualities, by writing:

> ... one must follow the "Universal Balance" ... that is, the Divine guidance which God has revealed through the prophets. Only in this way can man bring his beliefs, his thoughts, and his activities into conformity with the Divine Form upon which he was created. Ibn al-'Arabī' often refers to the Universal Balance as the Balance of the Law...revealed by God and exemplified in its highest form through the Koran and the example of Muhammad. Only the external, formal, particular pronouncements of God can protect man from his own egocentric ignorance... Only a norm revealed by God Himself can allow man to assume God's character traits and names.[74]

Chittick goes on to explain that, paradoxically, these laws and norms are not meant for humans to become God-like; rather, they are intended to efface the individual self until there is nothing left except that which truly exists: the Divine Form.[75] In other words, the process of acquiring the virtues requires the negation of the human self-ego so that the Heart assumes God's Divine Names and Qualities. What is interesting, however, is that some of God's Names and Qualities seem to oppose each other. For example, in the Quran, God reveals Himself as both the Merciful and the Just; the Immanent and the Transcendent; and the Giver and the Taker. The Islamic intellectual tradition captures these differences by separating God's Names into two groups. The first group is the Names of transcendence, majesty, or masculinity. These include names such as the Wise, and the Just. The second group is the Names of immanence, beauty, or femininity. These include names such as the Kind, and the Merciful.[76] It is important to note that these differences only exist in God at the level of being, that is, at level of revelation or creation.[77] According to the school of Islamic traditionalism, the apparently contradictory Names of

---

[73] *The Peak*, Number 324.
[74] William Chittick, "Introduction" to *The Name and the Named*, by Shaykh Tosun Bayrak al-Jerrahi al-Halveti (Louisville: Fons Vitae, 2000), 20.
[75] Chittick, "Introduction," 22.
[76] Chittick, ed., *Esssential Seyyed Hossein Nasr*, 77.
[77] At the level of beyond-being, God's is considered to be absolute unity, beyond all dichotomy.

God are manifested in the cosmos as a synthesis of polarities that result in complete balance or harmony. For example, the Quran states:

> And We spread out the earth, and cast in it firm mountains, and We grew in it every kind of balanced thing, (15:19)

> ...the herb and the tree prostrate [to Allah]. He raised the heaven high and set up the balance, declaring, 'Do not infringe the balance! Maintain the weights with justice, and do not shorten the balance!' (55:07-09)

> He created seven heavens in layers. You do not see any discordance in the creation of the All-beneficent. Look again! Do you see any flaw? Look again, once more. Your look will return to you humbled and weary. (67:03-04)

It is in this light that Nasr describes the 'rhythms of Muslim life' in an Islamic society:

> for Muslims the whole universe consists of the reflection in various combinations of the Divine Names, and human life is lived amid the polarizations and tensions as well as harmony of the cosmic and human qualities derived from these Names.[78]

According to the school of Islamic traditionalism, this harmony or balance is the imprint of God's oneness on His creation.[79] Thus, each individual, like the cosmos as a whole, is able to exist and function in harmony by synthesizing the different Names and Qualities of God within themselves. From this metaphysical perspective, humans are whole unto themselves; each has the *potential* 'to be' virtuous and complete. However, it is extremely important to point out that, from the worldly perspective, human beings are created with different natures, norms, and aptitudes. According to Muslim traditionalists, these differences are a product of God's wisdom and also essential to the human state.[80] Thus, it is only through understanding, situating, and embracing these differences – in accordance with the revealed law and its Divine norms – that people can create harmonious selves, families, and

---

[78] Chittick, ed., *Essential Seyyed Hossein Nasr*, 77.
[79] Nasr, *Heart of Islam*, 243.
[80] Nasr, *Islam in the Modern*, 63.

societies, as well as actualize their potential as theomorphic beings. Nasr points out:

> Transcending the Law in Islam in the direction of the Spirit has never been though the flouting of the Law, through breaking or denying its formal structure, but by transcending it from within... To speak of Islam on the level of individual and social practice is to speak of the *Sharī'ah*, which has provided over the centuries guidelines for those who have wanted or wish today to live according to God's Will in its Islamic form.[81]

This necessity of embracing God-given differences and norms is addressed in the following chapter. For now, it is important to conclude this chapter by asking the following question: how exactly does this theory of spiritual virtue connect to ethics?

In the Quran, God manifests different Names and Qualities on the terrestrial realm depending on His absolute knowledge as well as the particular circumstances of any given situation. For example, at times, God turns towards His creatures in mercy, and, at other times, He turns towards them in judgement:

> Again you turned away after that; and were it not for Allah's grace on you and His mercy, you would have surely been among the losers. (2:64)

> as in the case of Pharaoh's clan and those who were before them, who denied Our signs. So Allah seized them for their sins, and Allah is severe in retribution. (3:11)

These differences are the result of the fact that morality operates on the terrestrial plane; thus, it must take into account the latter's differentiated, relative, and ephemeral nature. Similarly, a virtuous heart functions as a microcosmic Divine guide that allows one to act ethically in a world of change and becoming. In other words, it is the virtue that gives morality its transcendent authority, and its ability to correctly judge between right and wrong. If there is no virtue, then morals are cut from their heavenly source, and laws simply become constructed moralities based on sentiment with no ground in objective truth. In explaining this relationship, Tage Lindbom writes that

---

[81] Nasr, *Heart of Islam*, 119.

Virtue stands thus "midway" between God and moral imperatives. It is virtue...that gives men their scale of moral values and their standards of behavior, and virtue must take precedence over morality, defining and determining it. But it is not...an outward ordinance of acts and attitudes. Its life is an inward one... In this sense, virtue is ontological reintegration, not the product of subjective aspirations.[82]

Thus, according to Islamic traditionalism, it is both virtue and revelation that work together to decide the right course of action in any particular situation.[83] In the words of Schuon:

> ...there are two poles for the manifestation of Divine Wisdom and they are: firstly, the Revelation "above us" and secondly, the Intellect "within us"; the Revelation provides the symbols while the Intellect deciphers them and "recollects" their content... Revelation is an unfolding and Intellect a concentration; the descent coincides with the ascent.[84]

An interesting example of this ethical perspective can be found in the Quranic narrative relating to the meeting between Moses and Khidr. According to this narrative, Khidr was a chosen servant of God who was blessed with knowledge of the Heart. Wanting to learn from him, Moses asked: "May I follow you for the purpose that you teach me some of the probity you have been taught?"[85] Khidr was hesitant and responded: "...Indeed you cannot have patience with me! And how can you have patience about something you do not comprehend?"[86] Upon hearing this, Moses promised to be patient, obedient, and accept Khidhr's actions without question or objection. Nevertheless, on three different occasions, Moses was unable to stay silent. Hence, Khidhr told his companion: "...This is where you and I shall part. I will inform you about the interpretation of that over which you could not maintain patience."[87] Khidhr explained that – despite outward appearances – the unseen realities of his actions were good and

---

[82] Tage Lindbom, "Virtue and Morality," in *The Underlying Religion: An Introduction to the Perennial Philosophy*, ed. Martin Lings and Clinton Minnaar (Bloomington: World Wisdom, 2006), 286.

[83] According to Muslim traditionalists, virtue is not a substitution for revelation in general, and Islamic law in particular. Rather, Islamic law and virtue are self-reflexive, that is, they reinforce and orient each other.

[84] Schuon, *Understanding Islam*, 48.

[85] 18:66.

[86] 18:67-68.

[87] 18:78.

in accordance with God's will and the Divine law. In the context of this narrative, Moses represents the tradition of deontological ethics and Khidr represents the tradition of virtue ethics. Khidr – a transformed soul – was able to discern right from wrong using his inward and microcosmic Divine guide. According to this perspective of virtue ethics, today's 'religious moralities' generally make the error of assuming moral laws are absolute and universal. On the other hand, today's 'secular moralities' generally make the error of ignoring the absolute principles behind particular laws.[88] The former leads to religious dogmatism and the latter leads to secular relativity. In this regard, Schuon's poetry reads:

> One Should not confuse true virtue
> With morality —purely outward acts
> That change with land and custom,
> And do not transform the substance of the soul.
>
> Virtue is inward — it resides in the nature
> Of things; its values are the same
> From people to people, and in every religion;
> Humility magnanimity and devotion are the paths
>
> That lead from the earthly world to heaven[89]

In relation to individuals then, the purpose of existence is to serve and represent God by manifesting or reflecting His Divine Names and Qualities in balance. In doing so, the human being is able to understand the principles behind the revealed law and, thereby, interpret and apply those laws without sliding into moral dogmatism or moral relativity. It is important to note that all people are not 'naturally inclined' to pursue the goal of human perfection. Nonetheless, the point remains: Muslims believe in God and His revelation, and they understand that they are tasked with knowing the truth and acting ethically. As I demonstrate in the next chapter, this particular Muslim understanding of life is sometimes at odds with the secular-liberal conception of human rights and the cause of friction between the two worldviews.

---

[88] Both the traditionalist and progressive schools would agree with this statement in general. However, they would disagree concerning what is absolute and universal and what is relative and contingent.

[89] Frithjof Schuon, *Songs Without Names: Volumes I-VI* (Bloomington: World Wisdom, 2006), 279.

Chapter 6

Virtue Theory and its Implications for Human Rights

This final chapter engages in a critical discussion concerning the general implications of Islamic virtue ethics in the area of human rights. This is followed by some introductory remarks concerning the specific issues of Islamic law, religious pluralism, corporeal punishment, and gender. First, however, it is important to reiterate why it is important to understand 'Islamic traditionalism' even though traditional societies – largely due to colonization and globalization – no longer exist today. First, the traditional Islamic worldview, which has characterized the general Muslim mentality for over a thousand years, is still very much alive today. Thus, Muslims are more inclined to adopt 'new' concepts if they understand them as part and parcel of their religious heritage. Second, the de-secularization of some societies and the rise of so-called 'Islamism' means the possibility of an Islamic nation-state that is, at least to some extent, structured in accordance with traditional socio-legal and political norms. According to Adis Dudrija, The concept of Islamism "…emerged in the context of a modern, postcolonial nation-state in the Muslim majority world [and]… refers to political movements who oppose the authoritarian "secular" political establishments in the Middle East on the basis of some kind of "Islamisation" of society platform."[1] Duderija goes on to argue in favor of a 'progressive Islamism', that is, a form of political Islam that is based on progressive ideals; one that is "cosmopolitan in outlook, embraces constitutional democracy and contemporary ideas on human rights, gender equality and vibrant civil society."[2]

For Muslims, the objective and ultimate Reality behind everything – including human rights – is God. More specifically, it is God as He has revealed Himself and the His law in the Quran. This is why the Universal Islamic Declaration begins by stating:

---

[1] Adis Duderija, "Why I am a Progressive Islamist," ABC Religion and Ethics, accessed March 17, 2018, https://www.abc.net.au/religion/why-i-am-a-progressive-islamist/10096584.
[2] Duderija, "Progressive Islamist."

Human rights in Islam are firmly rooted in the belief that God, and God alone, is the Law Giver and the Source of all human rights. Due to their Divine origin, no ruler, government, assembly or authority can curtail or violate in any way the human rights conferred by God, nor can they be surrendered.[3,4]

This is important because it means that rights exist by way of sovereign authority and are not a set of constructed and relative moralities that are in a constant state of flux. Rather, they have the potential to be based on the perennial principles of a sacred text and the knowledge of a virtuous Heart. These principles, which can be found in virtually every religious tradition, have grounded and guided human collectivities for thousands of years. It would be arrogant to dismiss them as 'primitive' and think that they have little to offer the modern world.

6.1. Human rights and the station of servanthood

The way in which people understand reality and their purpose in life determines their intellectual and ethical ethos in general, and their understanding of human rights in particular. According to the Quran and Islamic intellectual tradition, Muslims are both servants and representatives of God on earth. However, as mentioned, it is the station of servanthood and the concomitant idea of human responsibilities that is primary in the Islamic worldview and general Muslim mentality.[5] This means that Muslims generally understand themselves, at least, first and foremost, as creatures who are responsible to God and this responsibility is carried out by following the revealed law. As I argue, it is this primacy of the station of servanthood that is the reason for much of the tension with the secular-liberal understanding of human rights.

The first and most obvious implication of the station of servanthood is that the contemporary focus on human *rights* is misguided. This is because it

---

[3] See "Universal Islamic Declaration."

[4] To be clear, I do not believe that the Universal Islamic Declaration is, or should be, representative of all Muslims and their societies. Again, I believe that there should be multiple human rights models across societies and within societies. My working assumption is that this inclusive and decentralized approach would curb the abuse of power and lead to an 'after-the-fact' consensus on the substance of universal rights.

[5] As mentioned, it is also the station of servanthood and responsibilities that lead to the station of representation and rights.

ignores or pays little attention to the duty or responsibility to serve God in the deepest sense of the word. The Qur'an states:

> And admonish, for admonition indeed benefits the faithful. I did not create the jinn and the humans except that they may worship Me. I desire no provision from them, nor do I desire that they should feed Me. (51:55-57)

> When We took a pledge from the Children of Israel, saying: 'Worship no one but Allah, do good to your parents, relatives, orphans, and the needy, speak kindly to people, maintain the prayer, and give the zakat,' you turned away, except a few of you, and you were disregardful. (02:83)

> 'Did I not exhort you, O children of Adam, saying, "Do not worship Satan. He is indeed your manifest enemy. Worship Me. That is a straight path"? Certainly, he has led astray many of your generations. Have you not exercised your reason? (36:60-62)

According to ibn 'Umar al-Zamakhsharī (d.1144), Quranic verse 51:56

> points to the purpose for which human beings were created, even if most of them do not fulfil this function. From this perspective, God only created human beings to worship Him by choosing to worship freely and not being constrained to do it, because He created them as contingent beings...[6]

Similarly, *The Study Quran* notes that the term 'enjoin' in verse 36:60 has the same root as '*ahd* meaning vow or covenant; therefore, "it relates to the covenant that all human beings made with God before coming into this world, for in acknowledging that God is their Lord, they acknowledge only He is worthy of worship"[7] In any case, these type of verses show that responsibility towards God and his creatures are at the core of the Islamic worldview. This is also why Imam Ali's sermons normally began by reminding his listeners to remember God and fulfill their duty to Him. For instance, in the Imam's famous correspondence with Malik al-Ashtar, he reminds the latter that his attitude and behavior towards his subjects in Egypt should be determined by

---

[6] Nasr et al., *The Study Quran*, 1280.
[7] Nasr et al., *The Study Quran*, 1080.

the remembrance of God and the understanding that all power and majesty belong to God alone:

> Do not set yourself to fight Allah because you have no power to meet His power and you cannot do without His pardon and mercy. Do not regret forgiving or being merciful in punishing… Do not say: "I have been given authority, I enjoy it when I order," because it engenders confusion in the heart, weakens the religion and takes one to his ruin. If the authority in which you are placed produces pride or vanity in you, look at the greatness of the realm of Allah over you and His might the like of which you do not even possess over yourselves…[8]

Accordingly, any theory of human rights in Islam needs to be understood and formulated as a theory of human responsibilities. This is the only way that it will be accepted by Muslims as an integral part of their own intellectual heritage. Moreover, it is important to point out that this perspective should not be difficult to implement for two reasons. First, this is because every duty entails a right and vice versa; they are two sides of the same coin.[9] For example, the duty to respect others corresponds to the human right to dignity and the duty not to commit murder corresponds with the human right to life. Second, in practice, secular nation-states enforce a number of laws wherein responsibilities precede rights. In this regard, Nasr points out that

> …Even in the modern West, in many cases responsibilities precede rights. For example, we have to be responsible drivers before we are given the right to drive on public roads and we have to accept the responsibility of mastering the laws of the land before being given the right to practice law. *In Islam, this relationship in not a matter of expediency, but of principle, and its acceptance dominates the cultural and intellectual landscape.*[10]

Some human rights theorists disagree with the existence of a correlative relationship between duties and rights; however, their argument seems to be based on semantics rather than actual fact. Moreover, as Alison Renteln points out, establishing this relationship is important insofar as it allows international human rights to be more flexible and inclusive:

---

[8] *The Peak*, Letter 52.
[9] This is known as the logical correlativity doctrine. In general, see Renteln, "Concept of Human Rights."
[10] Nasr, *Heart of Islam*, 278. (Emphasis added)

The importance of demonstrating the logical correlativity of rights and duties does not lie so much in any explanatory power it has for Western human rights theories, but rather in the flexibility it affords the formulation of international human rights standards. Correlativity is crucial because it means that the framing of moral claims in terms other than rights is not necessarily problematic. The recognition of an obligation may well signify the presence of an implicit right.[11]

Thus, Muslims feel at odds with any theory of justice that does not consider one's duty towards God as central and is solely focused on expounding all the different rights that humans have. On the other hand, the notion of duty or responsibility is already part of the Muslim worldview and can more easily be applied in order to further the cause of justice and peace in Muslim societies.

Another implication of the station of servanthood is that it is at odds with the modern-liberal understanding of liberty found in contemporary human rights' laws and norms. Of course, traditional Islam, both in theory and practice, allowed for individual freedom and distinguished between private and public acts. Thus, the issue is not about freedom in general; rather, it is about the type of freedom that is being emphasized. According to the school of Islamic traditionalism, this contemporary understanding of freedom misses the point of existence. This is because, according to the Quran and the Islamic intellectual tradition, freedom is mainly an intrinsic virtue and not an extrinsic state. In other words, freedom can be perceived in one of two ways. The first is outward, which is the freedom from bondage of the other. The second is inward, which is freedom from the bondage of the ego. In Lord Northbourne's words: "we can aspire to freedom *for* our terrestrial nature, or we can aspire to freedom *from* our terrestrial nature." [12] According to the Islamic intellectual tradition, it is liberation from the individual ego that is of the utmost importance because it is this type of freedom that is absolute in nature and has its roots in the Divine order. According to Lings,

> The desire for freedom is above all the desire for God, Absolute Freedom being an essential aspect of Divinity...It was clearly above all to this freedom that Christ referred when He said: 'Get knowledge, for

---

[11] Renteln, "Concept of Human Rights."
[12] Lord Northbourne, *Looking Back on Progress* (New York: Sophia Perennis, 2001), 5.

knowledge will make you free', inasmuch direct knowledge, Gnosis, means union with the object of knowledge, that is, with God.[13]

Of course, some may object on the basis that an individual must be free from external restrictions in order to overcome the oppressive nature of the ego. However, this is only a partial truth because one also needs external constraints, such as Divine laws, to actualize freedom on the spiritual plane. It is in this light that verses such as 5:6 can be understood:

> ...Allah does not desire to put you to hardship, but He desires to purify you, and to complete His blessing upon you so that you may give thanks. (5:6)

From another point of view, it is also a partial truth because there is no way to completely escape the ties of a relational and relative world; therefore, the concept of extrinsic liberty – and the importance placed on this right – is somewhat misleading. According to Northbourne:

> Progress achieved towards the satisfaction of terrestrial needs, desires and fancies contributes nothing by itself towards inward freedom; on the contrary, when pursues beyond what is necessary, it tends more and more to supplant and to suppress the search for inward freedom, thereby defeating its own ends.[14]

In the same light, The Imam also emphasizes the primacy and importance of inward freedom, that is, freedom from one's egoic self:

> The strongest people are those who are strongest against their own souls.[15]

> The ultimate battle is that of a man against his own soul[16]

Thus, from the Islamic perspective, the human right to freedom needs to be understood as a spiritual imperative. This is because freedom is one of the virtues that need to be cultivated in order to serve and represent God on earth. In this light, it is necessary for any Islamic human rights theory to place certain religious restraints on individual liberties. According to the secular-

---

[13] Lings, *Ancient Beliefs*, 40-41.
[14] Northbourne, *Looking Back*, 5.
[15] As quoted in Shah-Kazemi, *Justice and Remembrance*, 40.
[16] Shah-Kazemi, *Justice and Remembrance*, 40.

liberal tradition, these restraints exist at the point where the 'other' begins; according to the school of Islamic traditionalism, they exist from the outset, that is, at the point where the 'self' begins. Of course, following these religious restraints is generally an individual's prerogative as long as it does not infringe on 'others' pursuit of spiritual freedom. Nevertheless, the point remains: the over-emphasis on the secular-liberal understanding of freedom is generally alien to the Muslim intellectual and cultural orientation on a whole. As such, any Islamic theory of human rights would include some laws that restrain external liberty, and, in some cases, these restrains would be in friction with international human rights articles.

Another implication of the station of servanthood is that it is at odds with the modern-liberal concept of equality found in contemporary human rights' laws and norms. The school of Islamic traditionalism emphasizes the Divine dimension of equality over its worldly one. From the metaphysical perspective, equality is considered to be "the need to be adequate once more to the Divine Presence."[17] According to Lings, it is "...the greatest of all Mysteries [and] is expressed in Islam in the words: Neither My earth nor My heaven hath room for Me, but the heart of my believing servants hath room for me"[18] Similarly, Nasr writes that in an Islamic society, equality exists to the extent that

> All...are priests and stand equally before God as his vice-gerents on earth. But he who is more able to realize his real nature and function is qualitatively superior to one for whom being in the human state is only accidental. The equality of [humans] is not in their qualities...but in the fact that for all...the possibility of realizing their theomorphic nature and fulfilling the purpose of human existence is ever present.[19]

Thus, equality lies in the fact that every human has the potential to mirror God's Names and Qualities and reach the theomorphic state of the complete human being. However, as I have mentioned, from the point of view of the created order, this state can only be achieved by embracing the revealed law, Divine norms, and God-given differences. According to many Muslims today, the modern-liberal understanding of equality ignores the 'Divine balance' created by God, and it has a tendency to reduce things to their lowest common denominator. For example, the Quran states:

---

[17] Lings, *Ancient Beliefs*, 43.
[18] Lings, *Ancient Beliefs*, 43.
[19] Nasr, *Ideals and Realities*, 104.

> Is it they who dispense the mercy of your Lord? It is We who have dispensed among them their livelihood in the present life, and raised some of them above others in rank, so that some may take others into service, and your Lord's mercy is better than what they amass (43:32)
>
> And We spread out the earth, and cast in it firm mountains, and We grew in it every kind of balanced thing, and made in it [various] means of livelihood for you and for those whom you do not provide for. There is not a thing but that its sources are with Us, and We do not send it down except in a known measure. (15:19-21)

In the same light, Imam Ali is reported to have said the following:

> As soon as things came into existence, every one of them was allotted properties and their place in nature...Thus every creature and very object had a place permanently fixed, was assigned position in nature which none can change.[20]
>
> Be informed that people consist of classes who prosper only with the help of one another and they are not independent of one another...Allah has fixed the share of each one of them and laid down His precepts about the limits of each in His Book (Holy Quran) and in the Sunnah of His Prophet by way of a settlement which is preserved with us.[21]

According to Islamic traditionalism, people have different natures and, therefore, different Divine roles and 'callings'. On this view, hierarchal structures are a precondition for balance and harmony and do not necessarily lead to oppression.[22] According to Muslim traditionalists, it is the loss of hierarchy – based on Divine archetypes and human natures – that has replaced balance and harmony for disorder and chaos in the modern world. According to Guenon:

---

[20] As quoted in Lakhani, *Sacred Foundations*, 18.
[21] *The Peak*, 795.
[22] This is not to dismiss the undeniable fact that many Muslim women, for example, have been the victims of hierarchical power structures that have oppressed, silenced, and marginalized them. However, from the perspective of Islamic traditionalism, the answer can never be to destroy the 'Divine ideal' in favour of a 'human ideology'.

>...Under the present state of affairs in the Western world, nobody any longer occupies the place that he should normally occupy by virtue of his own nature... Since the undertaking of a function, no matter of what sort, is no longer dictated by any legitimate rule, the inevitable result is that each person finds himself obliged to do whatever kind of work he can get, often that for which he is the least qualified... It is the negation of these differences, bringing with it the whole negation of all social hierarchy, that is the cause of this whole disorder...[23]

Therefore, it is this specific understanding of equality and its preconditions that must take precedence in any theory of Islamic theory of human rights. Of course, as the section on gender shows, this can cause serious tension with certain human rights articles.

This book's brief discussion on the station of servanthood clearly demonstrates why there is friction between the Islamic worldview and the modern conception of human rights. For most Muslims, any theory of justice, that is, human rights, must be rooted in God's revelation, and expounded in light of Islam's principle imperative: to serve and represent God according to the Divine Law. In other words, according to the Islamic intellectual tradition, any concept of human rights must take into account the reality of God and the cultivation of virtue. This means that the existing friction with human rights is not about the concepts of rights, freedom, and equality as such; rather, the friction is about the primary and almost exclusive emphasis on the modern-liberal understandings of these concepts. According to the school of Islamic traditionalism, it can be argued that all laws, norms, and rights are valid rights only insofar as they allow humans to achieve their purpose of existence. Of course, many Muslims have, and will continue to, fall short of this ideal. However, it is a matter of degrees; the closer one is to self-realization, the closer one is to a harmonious self, family, and society. Again, harmony is considered to be the imprint of God's oneness in the realm of multiplicity, that is, creation. Moreover, the secular space is not a vacuum. It is always filled with a system of beliefs that influences human states and dispositions. Thus, in my opinion, a society is 'un-Islamic' to the extent that it is centrifugal, this is, it draws people away from their 'absolute centers', that is, their Hearts, and moves them towards their 'relative peripheries', that is, their thoughts and desires. This is the case with many of today's so-called secular spaces, which, in the name of external freedom and equality, are filled with the ideologies of individualism and consumerism. According to Islamic

---

[23] Guenon, *The Crisis*, 70.

traditionalism, societies that have lost sense of the Divine Presence and no longer function as a means to salvation are invalid. According to the Quran, communities that disobey and/or forget God are eventually led to ruin:

> How many a town We have smashed that had been wrongdoing, and We brought forth another people after it. (21:11)

> Are they better, or the people of Tubba', and those who were before them? We destroyed them; indeed, they were guilty. (44:37)

> Have they not regarded how many a generation We have destroyed before them whom We had granted power in the land in respects that We did not grant you, and We sent abundant rains for them from the sky and made streams run for them? Then We destroyed them for their sins, and brought forth another generation after them. (06:06)

These verses should not be taken out of context to imply that the Quran is irrationally intolerant and violent. Rather, they should be understood as an expression of the perennial principle of justice: any society that turns away from the Real and chases the illusionary will inevitably be ruined. In any case, a society is 'Islamic' to the extent that it is centripetal, that is, it draws people away from the illusions of multiplicity towards the reality of unity. This is possible in a public sphere that is filled with reminders of the Divine; reminders of the human testimony of God's existence; and the human's acceptance of 'the Trust' to serve and represent God on earth by living according to Divine guidance. In this way, society functions as a 'silent theology' that indirectly guides it people. According to Lings:

> The purpose of religion as a whole is to knit together all looseness in man by setting up in his soul an impetus towards the center which will bring it once more within range of the attraction of the Heart... Here lies the essence of a sacred civilization, to be forever demanding...that it should pull itself together and keep itself together.[24]

Throughout Islamic history, religious law has been applied in different forms and to different extents. However, Muslim societies have always carried a palpable sense of the Sacred and the Quran and hadith have sculpted the thought and behavior of Muslims for over a thousand years. To reiterate, this cultivated Muslims mentality is the reason for much of the friction between

---

[24] Lings, *Ancient Beliefs*, 33.

the Islamic tradition and the contemporary human rights tradition. This friction is not simply theoretical; it has practical implications, and in terms of the latter, none is more controversial than the implementation of Islamic law.

6.2. Islamic law, pluralism, corporeal punishment, and gender

At the outset, it is important to restate that my goal is to explore the Islamic intellectual tradition – as explained by the school of Islamic traditionalism – in search of the fundamental principles that must ground any Islamic theory of human rights. More specifically, I am concerned with the Islamic notion of virtue, and its metaphysical implications in relation to the concepts of responsibility, freedom, and equality. Moreover, I have argued that a society is 'Islamic' to the extent that it is centered around the Sacred and functions to help human beings achieve their primary purpose in life. In this sense, Islamic law is only important insofar as it acts as a means for cultivating virtue and not as an end in and of itself. Nevertheless, it is important to briefly discuss some of the more specific issues of Islamic law in general, and its treatment of non-Muslims, corporeal punishment, and gender in particular. In doing so, I simply intend to provide some 'introductory thoughts' for the reader. As mentioned, this book is primarily concerned with virtue ethics rather than human rights as such. This is because, as I have argued, the former is the starting point and foundation of the latter.

According to the progressive school of thought, one of the greatest challenges facing the implementation of human rights – both in Islamic thought and practice – is the common Muslim understanding of Islamic law. Progressive Muslims generally argue that this particular understanding of Islamic law is based on three false assumptions. First, that the Quran's purpose is to govern rather than guide Muslim lives and Islamic societies; second, that the shariah is a Divine revelation rather than a human construct; and lastly, that humans have objective access to the Divine will and their duty is to simply accept and execute the law. For example, Khaled Abou El Fadl, writing on the subject of Islam and democracy, states,

> ...Arguments claiming that God is the sole legislator endorse a fatal fiction that is indefensible... Such arguments pretend that some human agents have perfect access to God's will, and that human beings could become the perfect executors of the Divine will without inserting their own human judgments and inclinations in the process.[25]

---

[25] Khaled Abou El Fadl, *Islam and the Challenge of Democracy* (Princeton: Princeton University Press, 2004), 9.

El Fadl goes on to write, "If we say that the only legitimate source of law is the Divine text and that human experience and intellect are irrelevant to the pursuit of the Divine will, then Divine sovereignty will always stand as an instrument of authoritarianism and an obstacle to democracy."[26] However, according to the school of Islamic traditionalism, this line of argumentation misunderstands the function of Islam in general, and the function of the Islamic law in particular. First, it is important to remember that Muslim traditionalists' understanding of religions is that they are all providential forms that embody different aspects of the Divine nature.[27] They are providential because different religious forms allow different 'types' of people to use their free will to choose any one of the 'paths that lead to the same summit'. In this light, Islamic traditionalism maintains that Islam and the shariah developed throughout history in accordance with God's will and by way of Divine wisdom. Second, Muslim traditionalists argue that something is 'Islamic' to the extent that it embodies Islam's doctrine of reality, that is, the doctrine of *tawhid*. Accordingly, they maintain that the shariah is an expression of the doctrine of *tawhid* because its all-encompassing nature functions to sanctify, integrate, and unify all human thought and behavior. It is important to note that this is one of the reasons for the friction between Islam and contemporary human rights. The latter generally assumes that human rights is solely a theory of justice and can remain neutral when it comes to the truth in general and religion in particular. Underlying this assumption is the fact that contemporary human rights are rooted in the Western legal tradition and its separation between the Church and state – a separation that never occurred in the Muslim world. Third, Muslim traditionalists argue that the comprehensive nature of the shariah does not remove human agency and free will, but, rather, it redirects it. In other words, Islamic law moves the will away from the horizontal or worldly aspects of life, and allows one to focus on the vertical or spiritual imperatives of religion. In this regard, Nasr writes:

> Some may object that accepting the shariah totally destroys human initiative. Such a criticism, however, fails to understand the inner workings of the Divine Law... Initiative does not come only in rebelling against the Truth...initiative and creativity come most of all in seeking to live in conformity with the Truth and in applying its principles to the condition which destiny has placed before man. To integrate all of

---

[26] Abou El Fadl, *Islam and the Challenge*, 9.
[27] For Islamic traditionalism's approach to Islamic law see Schuon, *Understanding Islam*, 1-35; 33-85. Also see Nasr, *Ideals and Realities*, 85-115.

one's tendencies and activities within a divinely ordained pattern requires all the energy which man is capable of giving.[28]

Furthermore, most Muslims have always understood that Islamic law is part and parcel of the human intellectual endeavor. For example, is seen in the fact that there are different but equally acceptable schools of law in Islam. However, at the same time, Muslims understand that this intellectual endeavor has its basis in the Quran and the latter's transcendent principles. This means that Muslims understand Islamic law as an extension of the Quran and, therefore, Divine in its own right, that is, in principle. For example, Mohammad Kamali points out:

> Although the Qur'ān contains specific rulings on such matters as marriage, divorce, inheritance and penalties, the larger part of the Qur'ānic legislation consists of broad and comprehensive principles. The specific legislation of the Qur'ān is often designed so as to make its general principles better understood. Being the principle source of the *Sharī'ah*, the Qur'ān provides general guidelines on almost every major topic of Islamic law.[29]

Moreover, as I have argued, Muslim traditionalists have always balanced the limitations of human subjectivity with the Islamic concept of transcendence and the human ability to know by way of revelation and virtue. Dismissing the concept of transcendence and 'objective access' is equivalent to dismissing the reason for existence itself – and ignoring humanity's greatest gift and potential. Hence, it is not that "human agents have perfect access to the Divine Will"; rather, it is that they have access to it in lesser or greater degrees. Of course, I am not arguing that Islamic legal scholars have always used revelation's perennial principles and illuminated Hearts to develop the law beyond their immediate and subjective realities. Rather, I am simply arguing that any objection to Islamic law that is *exclusively* based on the concept of subjective and contextual relativity is alien to the Islamic intellectual tradition as a whole; therefore, it is unlikely to succeed in its goal. Finally, it is worth pointing out that the idea that Islam needs to reform and 'catch up' with society is a modern concept and virtually non-existent throughout the history of Islamic thought. This is because Muslims have always sought to conform their societies to Quranic laws and norms and not the other way around. For

---

[28] Nasr, *Ideals and Realities*, 91.
[29] Kamali, *Shariah Law*, 20-1.

example, Imam Ali constantly reminds his listeners about the importance of following the revealed law. He states:

> ...This world begins in weariness and ends in death. You are accountable for what is lawful in it and punishable for what is unlawful... How excellent is the man who performs good deeds and undertakes acts of purity, who earns something he can set aside and avoided what he is warned against...[30]

> What can I say about a place in which the healthy fall ill and the sick are remorseful. Where the poor grieve and the wealthy are seduced, where one is held accountable for what is lawful and where unlawful things leads to fire.[31]

> The lawful and unlawful are distinct...The unlawful was not safe for past generations, and it is not safe for those yet to come...The law is inviolable.[32]

Despite the different understandings of Islamic law between the traditionalist and progressive schools, there is also room for some agreement and overlap. This is because Muslim traditionalists are also open to the idea of legal reform as long as this reform does not contradict the basic Quranic worldview and its fundamental principles. This is because they understand that the law operates in the world – the realm of the relative – and, therefore, the Quran's principles must be continuously reapplied according to changing circumstances. This is why I have repeatedly underscored that it is both revelation *and* virtue that allows one to understand and execute the Divine Will as objectively as possible. For example, it is possible to argue that the Quran's specific laws of inheritance – wherein men are entitled to a greater share than women – are an expression of the Quran's perennial principle of justice. This is because, in most premodern Muslim societies, men were financially responsible for maintaining their families. However, in the context of modern societies where both men and women often carry the financial burden together, it can be argued that this particular expression of justice, that is, the shares of inheritance, is open to reform. Finally, it is important to conclude this section

---

[30] Whitall, *Treasury of Virtues*, 45.
[31] Whitall, *Treasury of Virtues*, 47.
[32] Whitall, *Treasury of Virtues*, 157. The full quote clearly shows that the Imam is speaking in relation to the Quran's concrete injunctions. He refers to the separation between men and women, marriage between relatives, and marriage to multiple wives.

on Islamic law in general by restating that traditional Islamic societies and traditional Islamic legal systems are virtually non-existent today. This is because contemporary Muslim nation-states are generally governed by modern socio-political institutions and modes of discourse, and they are not properly grounded in the premodern Islamic intellectual and ethical ethos as a whole.[33]

Another area of contention between Islam and human rights concerns the issue of pluralism. More specifically, it concerns the differential and oppressive treatment of non-Muslims. Certain Quranic verses and Islamic historical norms, *potentially* provide the ground for the marginalization and oppressive treatment of the 'Other'. For example, chapter four raised the issue of *jizyah* based on the following Quranic verse:

> Fight those who do not have faith in Allah nor [believe] in the Last Day, nor forbid what Allah and His Apostle have forbidden, nor practise the true religion, from among those who were given the Book, until they pay the tribute out of hand, degraded. (9:29)

According to al-Rāzī, there are a number of Jews and Christians that affirm the existence of God and the hereafter. Nevertheless, he still maintained that the legal ruling (*hukm*), that is, to "fight them until they pay the tribute or *jizyah*," applies to all 'People of the Book':

> These [who believe in God] do not fall under [the description of this verse], but the requirement of the indemnity holds for them since it is said that, when an indemnity is required for some of them one says the same for all of them, since no one [that is, no jurist] holds the view that there is separation[34]

In other words, al-Rāzī maintained that it applied to all 'People of the Book' simply because there was no legal opinion to the contrary. According to *The Study Quran*, "This interpretation characterizes much of the mainstream of Islamic legal opinion on the matter."[35] In addition to this, there are many

---

[33] A detailed study of contemporary 'Islamic' nation-states is beyond the scope of this paper. For a comprehensive analysis, see Olivier Roy, *The Failure of Political Islam*, trans. Carol Volk (Cambridge: Harvard University Press, 1994).
[34] Nasr et al., *The Study Quran*, 513.
[35] Nasr et al., *The Study Quran*, 513.

other Quranic verses that can and have functioned to construct a mentality of Muslim superiority among the Muslim peoples. For example:

> Do not marry idolatresses until they embrace faith. A faithful slave girl is better than an idolatress, though she should impress you. And do not marry [your daughters] to idolaters until they embrace faith. A faithful slave is better than an idolater, though he should impress you. Those invite [others] to the Fire, but Allah invites to paradise and pardon, by His will, and He clarifies His signs for the people so that they may take admonition. (2:221)

> those who take the faithless for allies instead of the faithful. Do they seek honour with them? [If so,] indeed all honour belongs to Allah. (139) Certainly He has sent down to you in the Book that when you hear Allah's signs being disbelieved and derided, do not sit with them until they engage in some other discourse, or else you [too] will be like them. Indeed Allah will gather the hypocrites and the faithless in hell all together. (4:139-140)

It is verses such as these that have sometimes been used to justify the oppressive treatment of the 'Other'. However, in my opinion, these types of verses are not absolute laws; they are particular regulations that were intended for a society that was divided along religious lines and were frequently at tension in accordance with those divisions. However, in keeping line with the school of Islamic traditionalism, there are two questions that need to be asked: what are the underlying principles of the verses that seem to justify marginalization of non-Muslims? And, what are the different ways that these principles can be understood and expressed in light of changing circumstances? In this light, I argue that verses such as 9:29, 2:221, and 4:139-140 are based on the perennial principles of truth and justice and the Divine command for people and societies to conform themselves to these two virtues. In other words, these verses speak out against any person that knowingly denies the truth and attempts to thwart justice. This argument is strengthened when one understands 'unbelief' (*kufr*) in its etymological sense of intentionally covering up the truth with ungrateful arrogance. In explaining the meaning of *kufr*, Chittick writes:

> The original sense of the term *kufr* is to conceal something. People who are ungrateful conceal the good that has been done to them by not mentioning it. A person who has no faith conceals the self-evident truths of existence. *Kufr*, in short, is understood as covering over and a

concealing of the truths one knows. Hence...the term (ungrateful) truth-concealing.[36]

Thus, the distinction between the believer and unbeliever can be reformulated as a distinction between sincerity and hypocrisy. In other words, in today's world, which the perennial school of thought characterizes as an age of skepticism and confusion, it is those only those who *knowingly* deny the truth and obstruct justice that can be considered and treated as 'unbelievers'. Moreover, a corrective to the marginalization of the 'Other', can also be found in the Quran and its metaphysics of pluralism. In this regard, Eric Geoffroy writes:

> ... In Islam, God alone is One and unique, all that is other than Him, namely, His creation, is projected into multiplicity. However, the Divine mercy, which 'embraces all things' ensures that there is no rupture between these two levels...Thus, the recognition of Unicity (*tawhid*) that is required by the faithful Muslim, should, by direct implication, bring about in his consciousness the recognition of solidarity and interdependence of all realms of creation.[37]

In other words, and more concretely, the Quran contains a number of principles that can and have been used by Muslims to create socially inclusive communities. These include the ideas that all humans are children of Adam; that they share a single human nature; and that the people of the book and their respective religions are based on a single and primordial religion. In this regard, the Quran reads:

> So set your heart as a person of pure faith on this religion, the original nature endowed by Allah according to which He originated mankind (There is no altering Allah's creation; that is the upright religion, but most people do not know.) (30:30)

> Indeed the faithful, the Jews, the Christians and the Sabaeans—those of them who have faith in Allah and the Last Day and act righteously—they shall have their reward from their Lord, and they will have no fear, nor will they grieve. (2:62)

---

[36] Murata and Chittick, *The Vision of Islam*, 42.
[37] Eric Geoffroy, "Pluralism or the Consciousness of Alterity in Islam," in *Universal Dimensions of Islam*, ed. Patrick Laude (Bloomington: World Wisdom, 2011), 98.

In the same light, Imam Ali reminds Malik b. al-Ashtar that his subjects are also his brothers – either in faith or in humanity – and, therefore, he should treat them accordingly. The Imam counsels his governor with the following words:

> Habituate your heart to mercy for the subjects and to affection and kindness for them. Do not stand over them like greedy beasts who feel it is enough to devour them since they are of two kinds: either your brethren in religion or your likes in creation. They would commit slips and encounter mistakes... So, extend to them your forgiveness and pardon them in same way as you would like Allah to extend Hist forgiveness and to pardon you...[38]

Thus, the Islamic intellectual tradition contains the perennial principles that are needed in order to extend equal civil, political, and socio-economic rights to all of its citizens. This includes the right to freedom of religion and conscience because it is this freedom and its responsibilities that makes one quintessentially human. As the Quran states:

> There is no compulsion in religion: rectitude has become distinct from error. So one who disavows fake deities and has faith in Allah has held fast to the firmest handle for which there is no breaking; and Allah is all-hearing, all-knowing. (2:256)

> ... To you your religion, and to me my religion. (109:6)

However, it should also be noted that these rights are not inalienable. They extend to all citizens, but only on the condition that these citizens do not abuse their rights in order to disturb public law and morality. Thus, rights are not dependent on an individual's relationship with God; rather they are dependent on their impact on society at large. For example, an individual has freedom of speech as long as this speech is not hate-speech with the goal of causing insult, harm, and discord. In this light, Nasr writes:

> In modern society, the rights of citizens do not change whether those citizens fulfill their responsibilities toward God or even believe in God or not... Some in the West have contrasted this state of affairs with the situation in the Islamic world, and claim that, from the Islamic point of view, such persons would have no rights. This assertion is, however, not

---

[38] *The Peak*, Letter 52.

at all true. If certain Muslims fall into religious and intellectual doubt...their right to the protection of their life and property by society still remains as long as they do not...act against social norms and laws."[39]

Nasr goes on to explain that religious and intellectual doubt cannot negate a human being's rights because, according to the Islamic intellectual tradition, all human beings are creatures of God and contain the 'Divine Breath'. Moreover, during the course of their lifetimes, they may return to their belief in God and act in accordance with that belief.[40]

Chapter five pointed out that the current friction between the Islamic penal code and contemporary human rights is a matter of different worldviews and their primary assumptions. It argued that, according to the traditional Islamic worldview, corporeal punishment can function on an individual, societal, and spiritual level.[41] Moreover, according to this same worldview, the punishment of incarceration, which is practiced by many secular-liberal nation-states today, is decidedly 'un-Islamic'. This is because the Islamic intellectual tradition considers the family to be a single 'body' and a fundamental unit of society. However, many human rights advocates also agree that incarceration is problematic. Here, western-cum-global and 'Islamic' human rights have the ability to etch out a space of overlapping consensus. More specifically, they can find consensus in the concept of rehabilitation. According to Leonard Leswisohn, Muslim jurists generally agree that the Quranic 'eye for an eye' doctrine of retributive justice means "retributive justice as a *process of rehabilitation* rather than a cycle of violence of the sort common in the pre-Islamic tribal culture of revenge."[42] From the perspective of the Islamic traditionalism, rehabilitation can be grounded in the perennial principles of Divine mercy and human free will, that is, the human ability to reform oneself. For example, the Quran reads:

---

[39] Nasr, *Heart of Islam*, 280.
[40] Concerning the debate on the 'status of a sinner', see Khalid Blankinship, "The Early Creed," in *The Cambridge Companion to Islamic Theology*, ed. Tim Winter (Cambridge: University Press, 2008), 33-54.
[41] Again, this was not an argument in favour of the traditional Islamic penal code's use of corporeal punishment. Instead, was an argument about the ways in which worldviews work in the background to shape human attitudes and norms. Moreover, it maintained that the principles that underlie the Islamic penal code can be expressed differently, and in line with the changing conditions of society.
[42] Leonard Lewisohn, "'Ali ibn Abi Talib's Ethics of Mercy in the Mirror of the Persian Sufi Tradition," in *The Sacred Foundations*, ed. M. Ali Lakhani (Bloomington: World Wisdom, 2006), 127. (Emphasis added)

> Those who bear the Throne, and those who are around it, celebrate the praise of their Lord and have faith in Him, and they plead for forgiveness for the faithful: 'Our Lord! You embrace all things in mercy and knowledge. So forgive those who repent and follow Your way and save them from the punishment of hell. (40:7)

> When those who have faith in Our signs come to you, say, 'Peace to you! Your Lord has made mercy incumbent upon Himself: whoever of you commits an evil [deed] out of ignorance and then repents after that and reforms, then He is indeed all-forgiving, all-merciful.' (6:54)

The principle of mercy is also found in the teachings of Imam Ali, where he emphasizes the importance of love, kindness, and forgiveness. In this regard, he advises:

> Be good to whoever behaves badly towards you, and reward whoever is good to you.[43]

> An expert jurisprudent is one who does not cause people to despair of God's mercy, does not cause them to lose hope of refreshment from God…[44]

Thus, the Quran and Islamic intellectual tradition provide Muslims with the principles they need to incorporate rehabilitation into their legal systems without betraying the Quran's perennial principles and fundamental worldview. However, it is up to Muslims to decide how much to limit corporeal punishments in favor of rehabilitation based on the principles of mercy and human free will.

Since this chapter is concerned with providing some brief and introductory remarks, its discussion on gender is restricted to the male and female and does not address gender in its full spectrum and fluidity. 'The role of women' in Islam is arguably the most contentious and debated area in contemporary Islamic thought. According to most progressive Muslims, the different religious descriptions and prescriptions for men and women in the Quran were largely a

---

[43] Haeri, *Sayings and Wisdom*.
[44] Cleary, *Living and Dying*, 71.

matter of context and are no longer applicable today.⁴⁵ For example, Islamic law maintains that in certain cases in which a 'witness' is needed, one man is equal to two women. This is based on the following Quranic verse:

> O you who have faith! When you contract a loan for a specified term, write it down... But if the debtor be feeble-minded, or weak, or incapable of dictating himself, then let his guardian dictate with honesty, and take as witness two witnesses from your men, and if there are not two men, then a man and two women—from those whom you approve as witnesses—so that if one of the two defaults the other will remind her. The witnesses must not refuse when they are called, and do not consider it wearisome to write it down, whether it be a big or small sum, [as a loan lent] until its term. That is more just with Allah and more upright in respect to testimony, and the likeliest way to avoid doubt, unless it is an on the spot deal you transact between yourselves, in which case there is no sin upon you not to write it... (2:282)

Abdulaziz Sachedina summarizes the issue at state by asking, "Is the conditional commandment given for the specific situation in the Medinese society to be interpreted as an unconditional commandment, evincing the probable conclusion that regardless of whether a woman errs or not, her evidence is to be reduced to half of a man's evidence?"⁴⁶ After citing a hadith that seems to confirm the 'law of witnessing', Sachedina goes on to write:

> This and other similar hadith raise serious questions not only about the authenticity of these narratives that ignored the intertextuality of the daily details of the lives of women entrapped in male jurists' subjectivity and skewed vision of her social role; it also puts in doubt the claim by the pious for the validity and applicability of these legal rulings in all ages and at all times.⁴⁷

Thus, for Sachedina and other progressive-leaning Muslims, many of the Quranic restrictions placed on women – and further developed by the Islamic

---

⁴⁵ In general, see Omid Safi, ed., *Progressive Muslims: On Justice, Gender and Pluralism* (Oxford: Oneworld, 2003). Also see Charles Kruzman, ed., *Liberal Islam: A Sourcebook* (New York: Oxford University Press, 1998).
⁴⁶ Abdulaziz Sachedina, "Woman, Half-the-Man? The Crisis of Male Epistemology in Islamic Jurisprudence," in *Intellectual Traditions in Islam*, ed. Farhad Daftary (New York: I.B. Taurus, 2001), 171.
⁴⁷ Sachedina, "Woman," 173.

legal tradition – were based on the context of seventh-century Arabia; therefore, they need to be revisited and reformed today. On the other hand, according to the school of Islamic traditionalism, the differences between men and women are essential to the human state and cannot be overlooked as a biological accident. This is because both masculinity and femininity have their roots in the Divine principle of creation.[48] In this regard, Fatima Casewit writes:

> ...Every human being is created "in the image of God." However, human beings are of two types: man and woman, and since we are all created "in the image of God," our souls must be like mirrors reflecting the light of God. The supreme polarity of the cosmos, or the macrocosm, is reflected in the human soul, the microcosm. As human beings our souls reflect God's oneness. As men and women we reflect the supreme polarity: the Absolute and the Infinite, and we combine these two Divine aspects in the human state.[49]

According to this view, men and women are entitled to the same dignity because they have the same spiritual and moral worth. This is because all human beings have the ability to reflect God's Divine Names and Qualities, and, in doing so, return to their original and theomorphic selves.[50] However, according to Muslim traditionalists, this fact does not negate the importance of God-given gender differences, norms, and roles. This is for two reasons. First, as mentioned, it is only by embracing these differences that men and women are able to transcend their individualities and return to their original state. To requote Chittick's summary of ibn ʿArabī:

> ... one must follow the "Universal Balance" ... that is, the Divine guidance which God has revealed through the prophets. Only in this way can man bring his beliefs, his thoughts, and his activities into conformity with the Divine Form upon which he was created. Ibn al-ʿArabī' often refers to the Universal Balance as the Balance of the Law...revealed by God and exemplified in its highest form through the

---

[48] Murata, *The Tao*, 14.
[49] Fatima J. Casewit, "Islamic Cosmological Concepts of Femininity and the Modern Feminist Movement," World Wisdom, accessed April 5, 2019, http://traditionalhikma.com/wp-content/uploads/2015/02/Islamic-Cosmological-Concepts-of-Femininity-and-the-Modern-Feminist-Movement-by-Jane-Fatima-Casewit.pdf
[50] Maria M. Dakake, "'Walking Upon the Path of God Like Men'? Women and the Feminine in the Islamic Mystical Tradition," World Wisdom, accessed April 25, 2019, http://www.worldwisdom.com/uploads/pdfs/64.pdf

Koran and the example of Muhammad. Only the external, formal, particular pronouncements of God can protect man from his own egocentric ignorance... Only a norm revealed by God Himself can allow man to assume God's character traits and names.[51]

Second, according to the Islamic intellectual tradition, families are a single unit and a fundamental building block of society. Therefore, men and women were created with different but complementary natures, norms, and roles so that they could live in peace and harmony with one another. In this regard, Casewit points out:

> One of the most important innovations of Islamic legislation was to restore the dignity and rights of women as responsible human beings, as individual souls standing before God. Whilst Islam emphasizes the rights and duties of all human beings towards God the Creator, woman is honored in Islam as the bearer of life and the pivot of the family unit. Her God-given function as spouse, mother, nurturer, and teacher of her children is vital for a stable society. The value of this essential function has been called into question in our times...[52]

From this perspective, neither sex is complete without the other, and neither sex is 'lesser' than the other.[53] With this being said, throughout Islamic history, the differences between the two genders have been expressed in a myriad of ways and these expressions are not problematic as long as they do not lead to the negation of God-given differences and any consequent disequilibrium. Of course, many premodern Muslim scholars, especially in the field of law, took an extremely rigid stance on gender and did not sufficiently consider the fluidity between the sexes and within each sex. Thus, in my opinion, it is clear that any 'reformed' Islamic laws on gender need to provide flexibility whilst keeping the Quranic worldview and its principles intact.

It is also important to point out that in modern societies today, many traditional Islamic laws regarding the male and female are practically impossible to apply. Nevertheless, the Islamic intellectual tradition's general understanding of gender is at odds with its modern counterpart, and the

---

[51] Chittick, "Introduction," 20.

[52] Casewit, "Islamic Cosmological Concepts."

[53] Again, it is important to note that my intention is not to dismiss or justify the oppression that Muslim women have undoubtedly faced throughout Islamic history. Rather, it is to explain the perennial principles that underlie the traditional Muslim understanding of the relationship between men and women.

friction between the two seems insurmountable. It seems this way because the progressive school's emphasis on 'context' and 'subjectivity' is not enough to displace the common Muslim understanding that the Divine Will created men and women with different and complementary roles for the sake of balance and harmony. This perspective is in line with the Islamic intellectual tradition and any effective reform must also be in line with the latter. In this light, and in my opinion, the most important work being done on the subject is by Muslim women such as Sadiyya Shaikh. This is because she is "rethinking the terms of the debate" by focusing on "theological anthropology."[54] Shaikh outlines her project in the area of gender ethics in the following way:

> In this chapter, I suggest that bringing particular Sufi perspectives to debates on gender in the law offers Muslim feminists rich spaces to explore the underlying foundations of the law. Such a project directs one's inquiry to core definitions of the human being, the God–human relationship and related implications for social ethics, all of which implicitly underlie fiqh discussions. I argue that this level of enquiry allows Muslims to re-examine critically the formulation of the fiqh canon in light of the deepest existential and religious priorities in the Muslim tradition. Such an approach provides important criteria to determine whether dominant fiqh concepts reflect the best possible contemporary understandings of essential religious and spiritual prerogatives in Islam.[55]

Although I disagree with Shaikh's conclusions, this type of approach from the progressive school may bring about some common ground in the area of gender. However, if this possibility does not become a reality, then human rights advocates must remember that Muslims are self-understanding agents with the right to self-determination; they do not need to be saved. Any disagreements must be approached dialogically, and if all else fails, differences must be accepted on the basis of mutual respect. In this regard, Coomarswamy writes:

> Of all the forces that stand in the way of…a mutual understand indispensable for co-operation, the greatest are those of ignorance and prejudice. Ignorance and prejudice underlie the naive presumption of a civilizing mission… Before a world government can even be dreamed

---

[54] Shaikh's theological anthropology is not a reference to the modern anthropological study of religion. It is a reference to the Islamic understanding of what it means to be human and the consequences of that understanding.
[55] Shaikh, "Islamic Law," 107.

of, we must have citizens of the world, who can meet their fellow citizens without embarrassment, as gentlemen meet gentlemen, and not as would-be school masters meeting pupils...[56]

Finally, it should be noted that the Muslim world is currently in the process of understanding, debating, and changing their stances on some international human rights norms – including those related to gender. An undertaking that is hardly noticed, and much less discussed. Sachedina correctly points out that

> In the last three decades...there has been sustained interest in the foundations of the Universal Declaration of Human Rights and its compatibility with Islam. A number of books and articles in Arabic and Persian written by some prominent traditionalist interpreters of the Islamic revealed texts...underscore the attention and interest the international document has attracted...[57]

Again, Muslims are more than capable of determining what is in line with their understanding of the purpose of life. There have already been many changes implemented by Muslims themselves and there is no need for any 'intervention' based on an assumed and unfounded moral superiority. Moreover, a single society does not share a single set of views; in every community, there is discussion, debate, and mobilization. Tensions are inevitable and those tensions, in some way or another, are ultimately resolved.

---

[56] Ananda K Coomarswamy, *The Bugbear of Literacy* (Bloomington: Sophia Perennis, 1979), 125.
[57] Sachedina, *Islam and the Challenge*, 6.

Chapter 7

Conclusion

There seems to be a growing consensus that human rights are a set of universal norms that can easily be adopted and applied by all of the different cultural traditions around the world. However, in the first part of this book, I argue that this assumed 'universality' is highly problematic. This is because contemporary human rights, as formulated in the Universal Declaration and its offshoots, are clearly underpinned by the secular-liberal tradition that developed during the Renaissance, Reformation, and Enlightenment periods in the West; therefore, they are at odds with other cultural traditions that do not share the same worldview and consequent value-system. For example, many of these 'other traditions' tend to emphasize duties over rights, the group over the individual, and some form of personal reconciliation over procedural legalism.[1] Moreover, this assumed 'universality' is also problematic because the secular-liberal ethical theories that attempt to justify or 'ground' the existence of rights are 'unstable' and contentious and, therefore, vulnerable to claims of ethnocentrism and relativism. For these reasons, the forceful implementation of contemporary human rights is unjustified and a form of cultural imperialism. This is also why the formulation and implementation of human rights need to be more inclusive and decentralized respectively. If this is done, my working assumption is that it will result in a minimal overlapping consensus that is the product of an 'accidental universality'. This 'after-the-fact' approach would ensure that rights are organic to each tradition and not another play towards economic and/or socio-political domination. To this end, the second part of my book offers a theory of virtue ethics that has the ability to ground an Islamic vision of human rights. This is important because virtue ethics asks the larger questions related to the meaning and purpose of life, and it is the answers to these questions that ultimately determine what people consider to be human rights. Thus, I construct my theory of virtue ethics by drawing on Muslim traditionalists in particular, and the Islamic intellectual tradition in general. More specifically, I address three fundamental topics: the nature of reality; human nature and the Divine-human relationship; and the cultivation of virtue. In doing so, I argue that Muslims understand that God is the source of

---

[1] In general, see Sinha, "Human Rights."

reality and that they are tasked with serving and representing Him on earth through revelation and virtue. In any case, my theory of virtue ethics explains why there is friction between the Islamic and human rights traditions, particularly when it comes to concepts such as responsibility, freedom, and equality. I conclude the second part of the book by briefly addressing some of the more practical issues of Islamic law, non-Muslims, corporeal punishment, and gender. In the final analysis, I argue that these two traditions can find 'spaces of convergence' on the condition that they engage in open, honest, and equal dialogue. However, I also argue that there are spaces of divergence, and that these differences must be respected by human rights advocates. The following is a more detailed summary of each chapter.

In chapter two, I critically explore popular human rights histories because these histories are directly connected to how people understand and act in relation to human rights today. I argue that these histories are problematic because they share three basic assumptions that tend to lead to an exclusive and totalitarian understanding of liberalism and its theory of justice, that is, human rights. First, they generally assume that human collectives develop in a linear and progressive fashion; therefore, human rights is directly or indirectly presented as the final answer to humanity's search for justice. However, this belief in progress is no longer tenable today. For example, it can be argued that scientific, industrial, and technological progress have also led to individual, spiritual, and social regress. Second, these popular histories tend to assume that the world's religions acted as a 'historical stage' leading to a universal world order based on human rights. However, this assumption overlooks the fact that religions continue to play a central and active role in lives of millions of 'believers'. This is seen, for example, in the rise of the so-called 'religious resurgence' and contemporary 'Islamist' movements. Thus, to relegate religion to history is to discard an instrumental source of legitimization for human rights. Third, and finally, these popular histories generally assume that the Medieval age was a 'dark' and oppressive period in Western history. However, this is a gross and inaccurate overgeneralization. For example, as Norman Cantor points out, the Church and aristocratic system was directly responsible for astounding periods of growth in agriculture, philosophy, and the arts during the Medieval period.[2] Thus, chapter two demystifies popular beliefs about the history of human rights. This is only in this way that a space can be opened up for alternative visions. The need to open up an inclusive space is also the reason that chapter three

---

[2] In general, see Cantor, *Inventing the Middle Ages*.

critically explores ethical theories that claim to 'ground' or justify the existence and substance of human rights.

Chapter three argues that human rights are normative claims that need to be justified in order to be accepted by all peoples around the world. To this end, I analyze three of the most popular ethical theories that attempt to ground human rights in a universal manner. These are the theories of utilitarianism, natural rights, and ethical sentimentalism. In terms of utilitarianism, I argue that it is problematic for three interconnected reasons. First, it assumes that it is possible to know all the various effects that are produced by human actions and, thereby, calculate what is moral and immoral. Second, utilitarianism assumes that peoples with different belief systems can agree on what constitutes 'human utility' in general, and 'levels of utility' in particular. Lastly, utilitarianism assumes that it is possible to measure and grade qualitative experiences in quantitative terms. To put it simply, all three of these assumptions are impossible to put into practice. Therefore, the moral theory of utilitarianism cannot justify the existence and substance of human rights. After exploring utilitarianism, I proceed to examine natural rights theories and argue they are also problematic. This is for two main reasons. First, modern natural rights theories, which can be traced back to John Locke and his imaginative 'state of nature', assume that human nature and human reason are universal. However, human reason and nature do not operate in a vacuum; they are largely determined by a people's culture and its respective beliefs, values, and experiences. Second, even if all people agreed on the constitution of basic human rights, they would undoubtedly disagree on the ways in which these rights should interact with each other – and with other rights —when put into practice. Thus, like utilitarianism, natural rights theories seem unable to effectively 'ground' human rights in a universal manner. Finally, in terms of ethical sentimentalism, its principal problem lies in its relative nature. If there is no 'objective foundation' for anything, then the same is true of human rights. This also means that what is 'a right' in one context may not be 'a right' in another. This obviously undermines the claim the human rights are universal, equal, and inalienable. Thus, the three most common ethical theories that attempt to justify human rights are problematic. Of course, these theories have their strengths and should be continued to be developed. Nevertheless, the point remains: all three are subject to ongoing debate within the secular-liberal tradition itself. Thus, there is nothing definitive about contemporary human rights and, therefore, there is no good reason to exclude alternative approaches. It is important to note that I do not argue in favor of a single human rights models. My working assumption is that multiple human rights models would lead to an 'after-the-fact' or 'accidental' minimal overlapping consensuses. In turn, this minimal consensus would make up a set of universal rights, and all other rights would be relative to particular societies.

After creating a 'space for dialogue', chapter four explores the specific issue of Islam and human rights. In doing so, I point out four principal 'spaces of friction' between the two traditions. These are the implementation of Islamic law in general; the marginalization of non-Muslims; the use of corporeal punishment; and gender differences. In looking at these issues, I also survey the general Muslim responses to these issues at hand and divide them into four broad schools of thought or tendencies: fundamentalist, liberal, progressive, and traditionalist. I mainly focus on the traditionalist and progressive schools because they are the most nuanced in their approaches, and because most Muslims can be placed somewhere in between the two schools. In any case, in chapter four, I argue that the progressive school's approach to reform is deeply problematic. This is because it exclusively relies on the socio-historical method – a method that is largely alien to the Islamic intellectual tradition and the Muslims that this tradition represents. More concretely, the progressive school is problematic because it has a tendency to negate aspects of the Islamic religion that many Muslims consider inviolable, such as the hadith literature or the shariah as a whole. Thus, in chapter four, I conclude that the progressive school will most likely fail in achieving its goal of reform. This is one of the reasons why I use the framework of the perennial school of thought in the Islamic context, that is, 'Islamic traditionalism', in developing my theory of virtue ethics. In my opinion, this is an important 'Muslim voice' that is generally underrepresented in Western academic institutions. Thus, for context, I conclude the chapter by situating the perennial school of thought within the larger field of religious studies.

In chapter five I argue that Muslim traditionalists, in line with the Quran and thought of Imam Ali, maintain that ethics are rooted in two sources: revelation and virtue. Thus, I develop a theory of virtue ethics by addressing three fundamental issues: the nature of reality; the nature of the human being and the Divine-human relationship; and the cultivation of virtue. This is important because it is the answers to these questions that ultimately determine what people accept as human rights. In developing my virtue theory, I argue that the goal of all human beings is to conform to God by serving and representing Him on Earth. Moreover, I argue that this is done through the acceptance of Divine laws and norms, as well as the cultivation of virtue. It is in this way that human beings are able to understand the principles behind the revealed law and, thereby, interpret and apply those laws without sliding into moral dogmatism or moral relativity.

For this reason, chapter five maintains that an 'Islamic human rights society' is one that is primarily concerned with spiritual transformation and aids Muslims in achieving their primary purpose in life.

Finally, chapter six explores the implications of the book's virtue theory in terms of human rights. It argues that there is friction between the Islamic and human rights traditions when it comes to the three fundamental concepts of rights, freedom, and equality. This is because the Islamic imperative to serve God and cultivate virtue means that Muslims tend to emphasize duties over rights; inward freedom over outward freedom; and spiritual equality over worldly equality. This doesn't mean that it is impossible to bridge the gap. For example, I point out that rights and responsibilities are correlative and, therefore, a theory of human responsibilities would necessarily and implicitly entail a theory of human rights. In any case, the chapter concludes by providing some introductory remarks concerning the issues of Islamic law in general, and its rulings in relation to non-Muslims, corporeal punishment, and gender in particular. In the case of non-Muslims, I argue that the Quran and Islamic intellectual tradition contain enough 'material' to create inclusive societies wherein people of different faiths can co-exist together without discrimination. In the case of corporeal punishments, I argue that, at the very least, a partial overlap between the Islamic and human rights traditions can be found in the concept of rehabilitation. This is because the Islamic worldview emphasizes the principle primacy of mercy; moreover, it believes in the concept of free will and the latter implies that humans have the ability to change. Finally, I argue that the issue of gender is the most problematic in terms of Islam and contemporary human rights. This is because Muslims tend to believe that men and women have been created with different Divine natures and norms so that they can live in harmony together as a single unit. Nevertheless, throughout Islamic history, Islamic law has always been expressed in different ways and to different extents. Moreover, Islamic legal scholars have almost always taken 'context'; into consideration before making any rulings. Thus, there is still room for change as long as the perennial principles of the Quran remain in place. Whatever happens, it is important to remember that Muslims, like all peoples, are agents with self-understanding and the right to determine what is and what is not in line with their worldview. Human rights cannot justifiably be forced onto any cultural tradition. This is why I believe the best course of action is the creation of multiple human rights models that lead to an 'after-the-fact' set of universal human rights.

Bibliography

Abou El Fadl, Khaled. *Islam and the Challenge of Democracy*. Princeton: Princeton University Press, 2004.

"African Charter on Human and Peoples' Rights." African Commission on Human and Peoples' Rights. Accessed July 10, 2019, https://www.achpr.org/legalinstruments/detail?id=49.

Al-Bukhari. Sunnah: Sayings and Teaching of Prophet Muhammad. Accessed April 1, 2017. https://sunnah.com/bukhari

Al-Jibouri, Yasin T., ed. *Peak of Eloquence: Nahjul-Balagha*. 7th ed. New York: Tahrike Tarsile Quran Inc., 2009.

An-Na'im, Abdullah, ed. *Human Rights in Cross-Cultural Perspectives: A Quest for Consensus*. Philadelphia: University of Pennsylvania Press, 1992.

———. *Toward an Islamic Reformation: Civil Liberties, Human Rights and International Law*. New York: Syracuse University Press, 1990.

"Asean Human Rights Declaration." Association of Southeast Asian Nations. Accessed July 21, 2019. https://asean.org/asean-human-rights-declaration/

Ashcroft, Bill, Gareth Griffiths, and Helen Tiffin, eds. *Post-Colonial Studies: The Key Concepts*. 2nd ed. New York: Routledge, 2000.

Baldwin, Thomas, ed. *G. E. Moore: Selected Writings*. London: Routledge, 1993.

Banchoff, Thomas S., and Robert Wuthrow. "Introduction." In *Religion and the Global Politics of Human Rights*, edited by Thomas Banchoff and Robert Wuthrow, 1-23. New York: Oxford University Press, 2011.

Barber, Benjamin. *Jihad vs. McWorld: Terrorism's Challenge to Democracy*. New York: Random House, 2010.

Barth, Karl. *The Theology of Schleiermacher*. Translated by Geoffrey Bromiley. Michigan: Eerdmans, 1982.

Bentham, Jeremy. "An Introduction to the Principles and Morals of Legislation." Library of Economics and Liberty. Accessed March 2, 2017. https://www.econlib.org/library/Bentham/bnthPML.html#anchor_n2.

Berajak, Rafik. "Purify." In *The Quran: An Encyclopedia*, edited by Oliver Leaman, 513-14. New York: Routledge, 2006.

Berger, Peter L., "The Desecularization of the World: A Global Overview." In *The Desecularization of the World: Resurgent Religion and World Politics*, edited by Peter L. Berger, 1-18. Washington: Ethics and Public Policy Center, 1999.

Blankinship, Khalid. "The Early Creed." In *The Cambridge Companion to Classical Islamic Theology*, edited by Tim Winter, 33-55. Cambridge: University Press, 2008.

Burckhardt, Titus. *Art of Islam: Language and Meaning*. Bloomington: World Wisdom, 2009.

Callaway, Rhonda L. "The Rhetoric of Asian Values." In *Exploring International Human Rights: Essential Readings*, edited by Rhonda L. Callaway and Julie Harrelson-Stephens, 112-22. London: Lynne Rienner Publishers, 2007.

Callaway, Rhonda, and Julie Harrelson-Stephens. "What are human rights? Definitions and Typologies of Today's Human Rights Discourse." In *Exploring International Human Rights: Essential Readings*, edited by Rhonda L. Callaway and Julie Harrelson-Stephens, 4-10. London: Lynne Rienner Publishers, 2007.

Cantor, Norman F. *Inventing the Middle Ages*. New York: Harper, 1991.

Casewit, Fatima J. "Islamic Cosmological Concepts of Femininity and the Modern Feminist Movement." World Wisdom Library of Articles. Accessed April 5, 2019. http://www.worldwisdom.com/public/viewpdf/default.aspx?article-title=Islamic_Concepts_of_Femininity_and_Modern_Feminist_Movement.pdf.

Casewit, Jane, ed. *Education in the Light of Tradition: Studies in Comparative Religion*. Bloomington: World Wisdom Inc., 2011.

Chittick, William C. "Can the Islamic Intellectual Heritage be Recovered?" Iqbal Academy Pakistan. Accessed December 7, 2017. http://www.allamaiqbal.com/publications/journals/review/oct98/2.htm.

———. *In Search of the Lost Heart: Explorations in Islamic Thought*, edited by Mohammed Rustom, Atif Khalil and Kazuyo Murata. New York: State University of New York Press, 2012.

———. "Introduction" to *The Name and the Named*, by Shaykh Tosun Bayrak al-Jerrahi al-Halveti, 11-25. Louisville: Fons Vitae, 2000.

———. *Science of the Cosmos, Science of the Soul: The Pertinence of Islamic Cosmology in the Modern World*. Oxford: Oneworld Publication, 2007.

———, ed. *The Essential Seyyed Hossein Nasr*. Indiana: World Wisdom, 2010.

Cleary, Thomas. *Living and Dying with Grace: Counsels of Hadrat Ali*. Boston: Shambhala Publications, 1996.

Clewell, Tammy. "Subjectivity." In *Encyclopedia of Postmodernism*, edited by Charles E. Winquist and Victor E. Taylor, 382. New York: Routledge, 2001.

Coomaraswamy, Ananda K. *The Bugbear of Literacy*. Bloomington: Sophia Perennis, 1979.

Dagali, Caner K. "Conquest and Conversion, War and Peace in the Quran." In *The Study Quran: A New Translation and Commentary*, edited by Seyyed Hossein Nasr, Caner K. Dagli, Maria Massi Dakake, Joseph E. B. Lumard and Mohammed Rustom, 1809-19. New York: HarperOne, 2015.

Dakake, Maria M. "Walking Upon the Path of God Like Men? Women and the Feminine in the Islamic Mystical Tradition." World Wisdom Online Library. Accessed April 25, 2019. http://www.worldwisdom.com/public/viewpdf/default.aspx?article-title=Women_and_the_Feminine_in_the_Islamic_Mystical_Tradition.pdf

Dalacoura, Katerina. "Islam and Human Rights." In *The Essentials of Human Rights*, edited by Rhona Smith and Christien van den Anker, 208. New York: Oxford University Press, 2005.

De Barry, Theodore and Tu Weiming, eds. *Confucianism and Human Rights*. New York: Columbia University Press, 1997.

Derrida, Jacques. *Writing and Difference*. Translated by Alan Bass. Chicago: University of Chicago Press, 1980.

Donnelly, Jack. "Human Rights and Human Dignity: An Analytic critique of Non-Western Conceptions of Human Rights." *The American Political Science Review* 76, no. 2 (1982): 303-16.

———. "The Relative Universality of Human Rights." *Human Rights Quarterly* 29, no. 2 (2007): 281-306.

———. *Universal Human Rights: In Theory and Practice*. 2nd ed. New York: Cornell University Press, 2003.

Driver, Julia. "The History of Utilitarianism." The Stanford Encyclopedia of Philosophy. Accessed January 2, 2017. https://plato.stanford.edu/entries/utilitarianism-history/.

Duderija, Adis. "Why I am a Progressive Islamist." ABC Religion and Ethics. Accessed March 17, 2018. https://www.abc.net.au/religion/why-i-am-a-progressive-islamist/10096584.

Eliade, Mircea. *Images and Symbols: Studies in Religious Symbolism*. Translated by Philip Mairet. New Jersey: Princeton University Press, 1991.

Emon, Enver M. *Islamic Natural Law Theories*. Oxford, Oxford University Press, 2010.

Esack, Farid. "In Search of Progressive Islam Beyond 9/11." In *Progressive Muslims: On Justice, Gender and Pluralism*, edited by Omid Safi, 78-98. Oxford: Oneworld, 2003.

———. *Qur'an, Liberation and Pluralism: An Islamic Perspective of Interreligious Solidarity Against Oppression*. Oxford: Oneworld Publications, 1997.

Feldman, Noah. *The Fall and Rise of the Islamic State*. Princeton: Princeton University Press, 2008.

Finlayson, James G. *Habermas: A Very Short Introduction*. Oxford: Oxford University Press, 2005.

Foucault, Michael. *Discipline and Punish: The Birth of the Prison*. 2nd ed. Translated by Alan Sheridan. New York: Vintage Books, 1995.

———. *Power/Knowledge: Selected Interviews and other Writings 1972-1977*. Translated and edited by Colin Gordon. New York: Pantheon Books, 1997.

Freeman, Michael. "Beyond Capitalism and Socialism." In *Human Rights and Capitalism. A Multidisciplinary Perspective on Globalisation*, edited by Janet Dine and Andrew Fagan, 1-24. London: Edward Algar Publishing, 2006.

———. *Human Rights: An Interdisciplinary Approach*. Cambridge: Polity Press, 2007.

Freud, Sigmund. 1933. "Lecture XXXV: A Philosophy of Life." Marxist Internet Archive. Accessed June 14, 2017. https://www.marxists.org/reference/subject/philosophy/works/at/freud.htm.

Friend, Celeste. "Social Contract Theory." Internet Encyclopedia of Philosophy: A Peer-Reviewed Academic Resource. Accessed April 22, 2017. https://iep.utm.edu/soc-cont/.

Gauchet, Marcel. *The Disenchantment of the World: A Political History of Religion*. Translated by Oscar Burge. Princeton: Princeton University Press, 1997.

Geoffroy, Eric. "Pluralism or the Consciousness of Alterity in Islam." In *Universal Dimensions of Islam*, edited by Patrick Laude, 98-105. Bloomington: World Wisdom, 2011.

Grippe, Edward. "Richard Rorty." The Internet Encyclopedia of Philosophy: A Peer Reviewed Academic Resource. Accessed August 10, 2019. https://plato.stanford.edu/entries/rorty/

Guenon, Rene. "Oriental Metaphysics." In *The Sword of Gnosis: Metaphysics, Cosmology, Tradition, Symbolism*, edited by Jacob Needleman, 40-57. Baltimore: Penguin Books, 1974.

———. *The Crisis of the Modern World*. Translated by Marco Pallis, Arthur Osborne and Richard C. Nicholson. Bloomington: Sophia Perennis, 2001.

Haeri, Fadhlalla. *Prophetic Traditions in Islam: On the Authority of the Family of the Prophet*. Translated by Asadullah adh-Dhakir Yate. Zahra Publications, 2016. Kindle.

———. *The Sayings and Wisdom of Imam Ali*. Translated by Asadullah adh-Dhakir Yate. Zahra Publications, 2018. Kindle.

Hallaq, Wael. *The Origins and Evolution of Islamic Law*. New York: Cambridge University Press, 2005.

Hare, R. M. *Moral Thinking: Its Levels, Method and Point*. Oxford: Oxford University Press, 1993.

Haykel, Bernard. "Salafis." In *The Princeton Encyclopedia of Islamic Political Thought*, edited by Gerhard Bowering, Patricia Crone, Wadad Kadi, Devin J. Stewart, Muhammed Qasim Zaman, and Mahan Mirza, 483-84. Princeton: Princeton University Press, 2013.

Heard, Andrew. 1997. "The Challenges of Utilitarianism and Relativism." Simon Fraser University. Accessed January 6, 2019. http://www.sfu.ca/~aheard/417/util.html.

Helminski, Camille, ed. *The Book of Character: Writing on Character and Virtue from Islamic and Other Sources*. Bristol: The Book Foundation, 2004.

Henkin, Louis. "Religion, Religions and Human Rights." *The Journal of Religious Ethics* 26, no. 02 (1998): 229-39.

Hinnells, John, ed. *The Routledge Companion to the Study of Religion*. New York: Routledge, 2010.

Hunt, Lynn. *Inventing Human Rights: A History*. New York: Norton, W. W. & Company, 2008.

Huntington, Samuel. *The Clash of Civilizations and the Remaking of World Order*. India: Penguin Books, 1997.

Ibhawoh, Bonny. "Restraining Universalism: Africanist Perspectives on Cultural Relativism in the Human Rights Discourse." In *Human Rights, The Rule of Law and Development in Africa*, edited by Paul T. Zeleza and Philip J. McConnaughy, 21-39. Philadelphia: University of Pennsylvania Press, 2004.

Ibn 'Arabī. *Divine Sayings: The Mishkāt al-Anwār of Ibn 'Arabi*. Translated by Stephen Hirtenstein and Martin Nottcut. Anqa Publishing, 2004. Kindle.

Ignatieff, Michael. "The Attack on Human Rights." *Foreign Affairs* 80, no. 6 (2001): 102-16.

Ishay, Micheline R. *The History of Human Rights: From Ancient Times to the Globalization Era*. Berkeley: University of California Press, 2004.

Jackson, Sherman. "Liberalism and the American Muslim Predicament." *The Islamic Monthly*, June 27, 2015. https://www.theislamicmonthly.com/liberalism-and-the-american-muslim-predicament/.

Jafri, S. H. M. *The Political and Moral Vision of Islam*. New York: Tahrike Tarsile Quran Inc., 2009.

Kamali, Mohammad H. *Shari'ah Law: An Introduction*. Oxford: Oneworld Publications, 2008.

Kant, Immanuel. *Grounding for the Metaphysics of Morals*. 3rd ed. Translated by James Ellington. Indianapolis: Hackett, 1993.

———. "Idea for a Universal History from a Cosmopolitan Point of View." Marxist Internet Archive. Accessed December 15, 2017. https://www.marxists.org/reference/subject/ethics/kant/universal-history.htm.

Kao, Grace Y. *Grounding Human Rights in a Pluralist World: Between Minimalist and Maximalist Approaches*. Washington: Georgetown University Press, 2011.

Kenny, Anthony. *A New History of Western Philosophy*. Oxford: Oxford University Press, 2010.

Khadduri, Majid. *The Islamic Conception of Justice*. Baltimore: John Hopkins University Press, 1984.

Kinsley, David R. *The Sword and the Flute: Kali and Krishna: Dark Visions of the Terrible and the Sublime in Hindu Mythology*. California: University of California Press, 1975.

Kolakowski, Leszek. "Marxism and Human Rights." *The MIT Press* 112 no. 4 (1983): 81-92.

Kruzman, Charles, ed. *Liberal Islam: A Sourcebook*. New York: Oxford University Press, 1998.

Kymlicka, Will. *Contemporary Political Philosophy: An Introduction*. 2nd ed. Oxford: Oxford University Press, 2002.

Lakhani, Ali M. "The Metaphysics of Human Governance: Imam 'Alī, Truth and Justice." In *The Sacred Foundations of Justice in Islam: The Teachings of 'Alī ibn Abī Ṭālib*, edited by M. Ali Lakhani, 3-61. Bloomington: World Wisdom, 2006.

Laslett, Peter, ed. *Locke's Two Treatises of Government*. Cambridge: Cambridge University Press, 1988.

Laude, Patrick. *Pathways to an Inner Islam: Massignon, Corbin, Guenon and Schuon*. Albany: State University of New York Press, 2010.

Lauren, Paul G. "History of Human Rights." In *Encyclopedia of Human Rights*, edited by David P. Frosythe, 394-406. New York: Oxford University Press, 2009.

Leaman, Oliver. "Sin." In *The Quran: An Encyclopedia*, edited by Oliver Leaman, 593-94. New York: Routledge, 2006.

Lewisohn, Leonard. "Ali ibn Abi Talib's Ethics of Mercy in the Mirror of the Persian Sufi Tradition." In *The Sacred Foundations of Justice in Islam: The Teachings of 'Alī ibn Abī Ṭālib*, edited by M. Ali Lakhani, 109-47. Bloomington: World Wisdom, 2006.

Lindbom, Tage. "Virtue and Morality." In *The Underlying Religion: An Introduction to the Perennial Philosophy*, edited by Martin Lings and Clinton Minnaar, 285-95. Bloomington: World Wisdom, 2006.

Lings, Martin. *Ancient Beliefs and Modern Superstitions*. 2nd ed. Cambridge: ArcheType, 2001.

———. "The Past in the Light of the Present and the Rhythms of Time." In *The Underlying Religion: An Introduction to the Perennial Philosophy*, edited by Martin Lings and Clinton Minnaar, 35-54. Bloomington: World Wisdom, 2006.

Lings, Martin and Clinton Minnaar, eds. *The Underlying Religion: An Introduction to the Perennial Philosophy*. Bloomington: World Wisdom, 2007.

Loomba, Ania. *Colonialism/Postcolonialism*. 2nd ed. New York: Routledge, 2005.

MacIntyre, Alasdair. *After Virtue: A Study in Moral Theory*. 3rd ed. Indiana: University of Notre Dame Press, 2007.

Manji, Irshad. *The Trouble with Islam Today: A Wake-up Call for Honesty and Change*. Toronto: Random House Canada, 2003.

Maritian, Jacques. *Man and the State*. Washington, D.C.: The Catholic University of America Press, 1951.

Mayer, Ann E. *Islam and Human Rights: Tradition and Politics*. 3rd ed. Colorado: Westview Press, 1999.

McCutcheon, Russell T., ed. *The Insider/Outsider Problem in the Study of Religion: A Reader*. New York: The Bath Press, 1999.

Mill, John Stuart. *Utilitarianism*, edited by T. N. R. Rogers. Dover Publications, 2007.

Minnaar, Clinton. "Introduction." In *The Underlying Religion: An Introduction to the Perennial Philosophy*, edited by Martin Lings and Clinton Minnaar, xi-xxi. Bloomington: World Wisdom, 2006.

Mitchell, Peter R. and John Schoeffel, eds. *Understanding Power: The Indispensable Chomsky*. New York: The New Press, 2002.

Morris, Clarence, ed. *The Great Legal Philosophers. Selected Readings in Jurisprudence*. Pennsylvania: University of Pennsylvania Press, 1959.

Morsink, Johannes. *The Universal Declaration of Human Rights: Origins, Drafting and Intent*. Pennsylvania: University of Pennsylvania Press, 1999.

Moyn, Samuel. *The Last Utopia: Human Rights in History*. Cambridge: Belknap Press of Harvard University Press, 2012.

Murad, Abdal Hakim. "Book review of Farid Esack's Qur'an, Liberation and Pluralism." Muslim View: Remagining British Muslims. Accessed February 14, 2018. http://masud.co.uk/ISLAM/ahm/esack.htm.

Murata, Sachiko. *The Tao of Islam: A Sourcebook on Gender Relationships in Islamic Thought*. Albany: State University of New York Press, 1992.

Murata, Sachiko, and William C. Chittick. *The Vision of Islam*. Minnesota: Paragon House, 1994.

Murray, Dale. "Robert Nozick: Political Philosophy." Internet Encyclopedia of Philosophy: A Peer-Reviewed Academic Resource. Accessed March 29, 2017. https://iep.utm.edu/noz-poli/.

Nasr, Seyyed Hossein. *Ideals and Realities of Islam*. Illinois: ABC International Group, 2000.

———. *Islam in the Modern World: Challenged by the West, Threatened by Fundamentalism, Keeping Faith with Tradition*. New York: HarperOne, 2007.

———. *Science and Civilization in Islam*. Illinois: ABC International Group, 2001.

———. "Scientia Sacra." In *The Underlying Religion: An Introduction to the Perennial Philosophy*, edited by Martin Lings and Clinton Minnaar, 114-40. Bloomington: World Wisdom, 2007.

———. *The Heart of Islam: Enduring Values for Humanity*. New York: HarperCollins, 2002.

———. "Who is Man? The Perennial Answer of Islam." In *The Sword of Gnosis: Metaphysics, Cosmology, Tradition, Symbolism*, edited by Jacob Needleman, 203-217 Baltimore: Penguin Books, 1974.

Nasr, Seyyed Hossein, Caner K. Dagli, Maria Massi Dakake, Joseph E. B. Lumard, and Mohammed Rustom, eds. *The Study Quran: A New Translation and Commentary*. New York: HarperOne, 2015.

Nathanson, Stephen. "Act and Rule Utilitarianism." Internet Encyclopedia of Philosophy: A Peer-Reviewed Academic Resource. Accessed March 13, 2017. https://iep.utm.edu/util-a-r/.

Nietzsche, Friedrich. *On the Genealogy of Morals and Ecce Homo*. Translated and edited by Walter A. Kaufmann. New York: Random House, 1989.

Northbourne, Lord. *Looking Back on Progress*. New York: Sophia Perennis, 2001.

Oh, Irene. *The Rights of God: Islam, Human Rights, and Comparative Ethics*. Washington: Georgetown University Press, 2007.

Oldmeadow, Harry. *Frithjof Schuon and the Perennial Philosophy*. Bloomington: World Wisdom, 2010.

Otto, Rudolph. *The Idea of the Holy: An Inquiry into the Non-Rational Factor in the Idea of the Divine and its Relation to the Rational*. 2nd ed. Translated by John W. Harvey. New York: Oxford University Press, 1950.

Outram, Dorinda. *The Enlightenment*. 2nd ed. Cambridge: Cambridge University Press, 2005.

Pals, Daniel L. *Nine Theories of Religion*. 3rd ed. Oxford: Oxford University Press, 2014.

Poerkson, Uwe. *Plastic Words: The Tyranny of a Modular Language*. Translated by Jutta Mason and David Cayley. Pennsylvania: The Pennsylvania University State Press, 1995.

Preston, Aaron. "George Edward Moore (1873-1958)." Internet Encyclopedia of Philosophy: A Peer-Reviewed Academic Resource. Accessed January 22, 2017. https://iep.utm.edu/moore/.

Qara'i, 'Ali Quli, trans. *The Qur'an: With a Phrase-by-Phrase Translation*. Translated by. New York: Tahrike Tarsile Qur'an, Inc., 2006.

Qutbuddin, Tahera, ed. and trans. *A Treasury of* Virtues *and One Hundred Proverbs*. New York: New York University Press, 2013. Kindle.

———, ed. and trans. *Light in the Heavens: Sayings of the Prophet Muhammad*. New York: New York University Press, 2016.

Qutb, Sayyid. "War, Peace and Islamic Jihad." In *Modernist and Fundamentalist Debates in Islam: A Reader*, edited by Moaddel Mansoor and Kamran Talattof, 223-47. New York: Palgrave, 2000.

Rahman, Fazlur. *Islam and Modernity: Transformation of an Intellectual Tradition*. Chicago: Chicago University Press, 1982.

Rawls, John. *A Theory of Justice*. London: Oxford University Press, 1971.

———. "The Laws of People." *Chicago Journals* 20, no. 1 (1993): 33-68.

Rayshahri, Muhammadi M, ed. *The Scale of Wisdom: A Compendium of Shi'a Ḥadīth*. London: ICAS Press, 2008.

Renteln, Alison D. "The Concept of Human Rights." *Anthropos Institute* 83, no. 4 (1988): 343-64.

Rorty, Richard. "Human Rights, Rationality, and Sentimentality." In *On Human Rights: The Oxford Amnesty Lectures*, edited by Stephen Shute and Susan Hurley, 111-35. New York: Basic Books, 1993.

Roy, Olivier. *The Failure of Political Islam*. Translated by Carol Volk. Cambridge: Harvard University Press, 1994.

Russell, Daniel C., ed. *The Cambridge Companion to Virtue Ethics*. New York: Cambridge University Press, 2013.

Sachedina, Abdulaziz. *Islam and the Challenge of Human Rights*. New York: Oxford University Press, 2009.

———. "Woman, Half-the-Man? The Crisis of Male Epistemology in Islamic Jurisprudence." In *Intellectual Traditions in Islam*, edited by Farhad Daftary, 160-79. New York: I.B. Taurus, 2001.

Safi, Omid. "Introduction: The Times are A-Changin' – A Muslim Quest for Justice, Gender Equality and Pluralism." In *Progressive Muslims: On Justice, Gender and Pluralism*, edited by Omid Safi, 1-29. Oxford: Oneworld, 2003.

———., ed. *Progressive Muslims: On Justice, Gender and Pluralism*. Oxford: Oneworld, 2003.

Said, Edward W. "Islam Through Western Eyes." *The Nation*. April 26, 1980. https://www.thenation.com/article/archive/islam-through-western-eyes.

Schuon, Frithjof. *Logic and Transcendence: A New Translation with Selected Letters*, edited by James Cutsinger. Bloomington: World Wisdom, 2009.

———. *Road to the Heart: Poems*. Bloomington: World Wisdom, 2003.

———. *Songs Without Names: Volumes I-VI*. Bloomington: World Wisdom, 2006.

———. "The Primacy of Intellection." *Studies in Comparative Religion* 16, no. 3 and 4 (Summer-Autumn 1984). http://www.studiesincomparativereligion.com/public/articles/the_primacy_of_intellection-by_frithjof_schuon.aspx.

———. *The Transcendent Unity of Religions*. 2nd ed. Illinois: Quest Books, 1993.

———. *The Transfiguration of Man*. Bloomington: World Wisdom, 1995.

———. *Understanding Islam: A New Translation with Selected Letters*, edited by Patrick Laude. Bloomington: World Wisdom, 2011.

Sedgwick, Mark. *Against the Modern World: Traditionalism and the Secret Intellectual History of the Twentieth Century*. Oxford: Oxford University Press, 2004.

Segal, Robert A. "Theories of Religion." In *The Routledge Companion to the Study of Religion*, edited by John Hinnells, 75-93. New York: Routledge, 2010.

Sen, Amartya. *Commodities and Capabilities*. Oxford: Oxford University Press, 1999.

Shah-Kazemi, Reza. *Justice and Remembrance: Introducing the Spirituality of Imam Ali*. London: I.B. Tauris Publishers, 2007.

Shaikh, Sa'diyya. "Islamic Law, Sufism and Gender: Rethinking the Terms of the Debate." In *Men in Charge? Rethinking Authority in Muslim Legal Tradition*, edited by Ziba Mir-Hosseini, Mulki Al-Sharmani, and Jana Rumminger, 106-31. London: Oneworld Pub., 2015.

———. *Sufi Narratives of Intimacy: Ibn 'Arabi, Gender and Sexuality*. Chapel Hill: The University of North Carolina Press, 2012.

Sharpe, Eric J. "The Study of Religion in Historical Perspective." In *The Routledge Companion to the Study of Religion*, edited by John Hinnells, 21-36. New York: Routledge, 2010.

Shestack, Jerome J. "The Philosophical Foundations of Human Rights." In *Exploring International Human Rights: Essential Readings*, edited by Rhonda L. Callaway and Julie Harrelson-Stephens, 21-27. London: Lynne Rienner Pub., 2007.

Sim, Stuart, ed. *The Routledge Companion to Postmodernism*. 2nd ed. New York: Routledge, 2005.

Sinha, Prakash. "Human Rights: A Non-Western Viewpoint." *Archives for Philosophy of Law and Social Philosophy* 67, no. 1 (1981): 76-91.

Smith, Huston. *Beyond the Postmodern Mind: The Place of Meaning in a Global Civilization*. 3rd ed. Illinois: Quest Books, 2003.

———. "Introduction" to *The Transcendent Unity of Religions* by Frithjof Schuon. 2nd ed., ix-xxvii. Illinois: Quest Books, 1993.

———. *Why Religion Matters: The Fate of the Human Spirit in an Age of Disbelief*. New York, HarperCollins, 2001.

Solon, Olivia. "George Soros: Facebook and Google a Menace to Society." *The Guardian*, January 26, 2018. https://www.theguardian.com/business/2018/jan/25/george-soros-facebook-and-google-are-a-menace-to-society.

Souroush, Abdolkarim. "The Evolution and Devolution of Religious Knowledge." In *Liberal Islam: A Sourcebook*, edited by Charles Kruzman, 244-55. New York: Oxford University Press, 1998.

Stelzer, Steffen A. "Ethics." in *The Cambridge Companion to Classical Islamic Theology*, edited by Tim Winter, 161-79. Cambridge: Cambridge University Press, 2008.

Stewart, Devin J. "Shari'a." In *The Princeton Encyclopedia of Islamic Political Thought*, edited by Gerhard Bowering, Patricia Crone, Wadad Kadi, Devin J. Stewart, Muhammed Qasim Zaman and Mahan Mirza, 497-505. Princeton: Princeton University Press, 2013.

Stoddart, William. "Mysticism." In *The Underlying Religion: An Introduction to the Perennial Philosophy*, edited by Martin Lings and Clinton Minnaar, 230-242. Bloomington: World Wisdom, 2007.

Tharoor, Sashi. "Are Human Rights Universal?" *World Policy Journal* 16, no. 4 (1999-2000).

"The Code of Hammurabi." Translated by L. W. King. Yale Law School, The Avalon Project: Documents in Law, History and Diplomacy. Accessed January 27, 2019. https://avalon.law.yale.edu/ancient/hamframe.asp

"The Declaration of Independence." US History. Accessed July 4, 2019, https://www.ushistory.org/declaration/document/

Trouillot, Michel-Rolph. *Silencing the Past: Power and the Production of History*. Boston: Beacon Press, 1995.

Tuckness, Alex. "Locke's Political Philosophy." The Stanford Encyclopedia of Philosophy. Accessed September 30, 2017. https://plato.stanford.edu/entries/locke-political/.

"Universal Declaration of Human Rights." United Nations. Accessed July 11, 2019. https://www.un.org/en/about-us/universal-declaration-of-human-rights.

"Universal Islamic Declaration of Human Rights." Al-Hewar Center. Accessed July 11, 2019. http://www.alhewar.com/ISLAMDECL.html.

Upton, Charles. *Legends of the End: Prophecies of the End Times, Antichrist, Apocalypse, and Messiah from Eight Religious Traditions*. New York: Sophia Perennis, 2005.

———. "What is a 'Traditionalist'? – Some Clarifications." Sacred Web: A Journal of Tradition and Modernity. Accessed July 25, 2017. http://www.sacredweb.com/online_articles/sw17_upton.html

Wadud, Amina. *Qur'an and Woman: Rereading the Sacred Text from a Women's Perspective*. New York: Oxford University Press, 1999.

Wells, Thomas. "Sen's Capability Approach." Internet Encyclopedia of Philosophy: A Peer-Reviewed Academic Resource. Accessed March 24, 2019. https://iep.utm.edu/sen-cap/.

Whitall, Perry N., ed. *A Treasury of Traditional Wisdom: An Encyclopedia of Humankind's Spiritual Truth*. 3rd ed. Louisville: Fons Vitae, 2001.

Winquist, Charles E. and Victor E. Taylor, eds., *Encyclopedia of Postmodernism*. New York: Routledge, 2001.

Zaidi, Ali Hassan. "Islam, Modernity and the Human Sciences: Toward a Dialogical Approach." PhD diss. York University, 2007.

Index

A

Africa, 51
   African Charter on Human and
      Peoples' Rights, 51, 53
Asia, 49
   Asean Declaration, 53, 62
   Asian values, 50
   Confucianism, 50

C

Christian natural law, 1, 20, 37, 38

E

Enlightenment, 22, 24, 27, 38, 59, 79, 153
equality, 133, 135, 137, 157
ethics, 4, 19, 31, 48, 100, 153, 155
   consequentialism, 100
   deontology, 103, 126
   Divine command theory, 103, 104
   ethical sentimentalism, 31, 43, 46, 47, 155
   natural rights, 31, 37, 38, 41, 42, 103, 155
   utilitarianism, 31, 32, 36, 155
   virtue, 4, 6, 11, 15, 106, 109, 121, 124, 126, 127, 153, 156, *also see* virtue

F

freedom, 131, 132, 133, 135, 137, 157, *also see* liberty
free-will, 113, 138

H

heart, 87, 105, 106, 117, 118, 119, 122, 124, 135
human nature, 39, 43, 46, 111, 113, 115, 134
human responsibilities, 15, 59, 116, 117, 128, 129, 130, 137, 157
human rights
   consensus, 1, 16, 21, 54, 55, 145, 153, 156
   ethical foundations. *See* ethics
   history, 14, 21, 24, 26, 29, 154
   Islam, 1, 2, 4, 15, 51, 100, 106, 107, 113, 130, 132, 135, 137, 138, 153, 156
   religion, 14, 15, 21, 26, 27, 57, 58, 59, 61, 154
   universality, 1, 3, 20, 21, 37, 42, 49, 51, 53, 153, 154, 155
humanism, 22, 59, 103

I

imperialism, 1, 15, 16, 20, 31, 153
intellect, 86, 87, 106, *also see* heart
Islam
   fundamentalist, 15, 72, 156
   liberal, 73
   progressive, 7, 15, 73, 74, 76, 77, 78, 137, 147, 156
   traditionalism, 5, 7, 11, 12, 15, 52, 62, 77, 89, 98, 110, 118, 122, 127, 131, 133, 135, 138, 142, 148, 156
   Universal Islamic Declaration of Human Rights, 52, 53, 127

Islamic law, 63, 64, 66, 67, 93, 94, 105, 137, 138, 149, *also see* shariah
   corporeal punishment, 15, 70, 71, 94, 137, 145, 154, 156, 157
   gender, 15, 67, 68, 99, 137, 146, 147, 154, 156, 157
   non-Muslims, 15, 69, 70, 137, 142, 154, 156, 157
   reform, 4, 8, 74, 77, 87, 95, 98, 107, 137, 139, 140, 150

K

Kant, Immanuel, 38, 39

L

liberty, 31, 39, 41, 131, 132, 133, *also see* freedom
Locke, John, 38, 40, 41, 155

M

modernism, 22, 40, 53, 55, 59, 94, 103, 118

N

names and qualities
   of God, 120, 122, 124, 126, 133

P

perennialism, 4, 5, 6, 78, 79, 81, 85, 86, 87, 88
post-colonialism, 54
postmodernism, 44, 46, 53, 54
Protestant Reformation, 21, 26, 53, 59, 79, 153

R

Rawls, John, 2, 40, 41, 54, 58

reality, 106, 107, 109, 110, 116, 117, 127, 156
religious studies, 82, 83, 85
remembrance
   of God, 114, 121, 136
Renaissance, 21, 26, 27, 59, 153
representatives
   of God, 115, 116, 126, 128

S

secular-liberal, 1, 3, 13, 19, 20, 21, 26, 38, 40, 42, 48, 49, 95, 117, 126, 128, 133, 153, 155
servants
   of God, 113, 114, 116, 126, 128, 131, 133
shariah, 63, 77, 138, *also see* Islamic law

T

tawhid, 109, 110, 122, 138

U

Universal Declaration of Human Responsibilities, 53
Universal Declaration of Human Rights, 14, 19, 20, 23, 40, 42, 52, 59, 60, 103
   drafting, 60, 61

V

virtue, 117, 120, 122, 125, 137, 139, *also see* ethics

W

worldview, 1, 3, 5, 6, 17, 19, 37, 45, 50, 52, 57, 62, 76, 79, 82, 93, 95, 98, 107, 127, 129, 135, 145, 153

www.ingramcontent.com/pod-product-compliance
Lightning Source LLC
Chambersburg PA
CBHW050638300426
44112CB00012B/1845